The Essential Guide for New Teaching Assistants

Second Edition

The Essential Guide for New Teaching Assistants provides an introduction for teaching assistants who have recently been inducted, or are going through the process of induction, and are working in schools with children or young people.

Giving teaching assistants an insight into the theories of teaching and learning and providing a background for understanding school processes and procedures, this new edition is fully updated to incorporate recent initiatives and changes in the National Curriculum. With an emphasis on personal responsibility and professionalism, the role of a teaching assistant and their relationship with qualified teachers is fully outlined.

Providing a comprehensive overview, chapters include practical guidance on:

- getting started in a teaching assistant role

- developing a reflective approach to personal and professional development

- the Every Child Matters initiative

- working in partnership with qualified teachers

- being part of a whole school team

- working with individual children to progress their learning and development

- further training and professional development.

Fully updated in line with National Occupational Standards, changes in the primary and secondary National Curricula and revised induction materials from the TDA, this book forms essential reading for teaching assistants seeking to understand the basic principles of education, teaching and learning.

Anne Watkinson is an educational consultant and experienced author dealing specifically with teaching assistants. She has had a wide and varied educational role, working as a teacher, head teacher and a senior school development adviser for Essex Local Authority. She worked with the then DFEE and DfES to develop the original induction materials for teaching assistants, and was involved with the development of higher level teaching assistants. She frequently gives talks, runs workshops and attends conferences across the UK.

The Essential Guide for New Teaching Assistants

Assisting learning and supporting teaching in the classroom

Second Edition

Anne Watkinson

Routledge
Taylor & Francis Group
LONDON AND NEW YORK

First edition published 2002
by David Fulton Publishers, and titled *Assisting Learning and Supporting Teaching*

This second edition first published 2010
by Routledge
2 Park Square, Milton Park, Abingdon, Oxon OX14 4RN

Simultaneously published in the USA and Canada
by Routledge
270 Madison Avenue, New York, NY 10016

Routledge is an imprint of the Taylor & Francis Group, an informa business

© 2010 Anne Watkinson

Typeset in Sabon by
Florence Production Ltd, Stoodleigh, Devon
Printed and bound in Great Britain by
the MPG Books Group

British Library Cataloguing in Publication Data
A catalogue record for this book is available from the British Library

Library of Congress Cataloging-in-Publication Data
Watkinson, Anne
 The essential guide for new teaching assistants: assisting learning and
 supporting teaching in the classroom/Anne Watkinson. – 2nd ed.
   p.cm.
   Includes bibliographical references and index.
 1. Teachers' assistants – Great Britain – Handbooks, manuals, etc.
 2. Education – Aims and objectives – Great Britain – Handbooks,
 manuals, etc. I. Title.
 LB2844.1.A8W379 2010
 371.14'124–dc22   2009025096

ISBN 10: 0–415–54710–5 (pbk)
ISBN 10: 0–203–86303–8 (ebk)

ISBN 13: 978–0–415–54710–9 (pbk)
ISBN 13: 978–0–203–86303–9 (ebk)

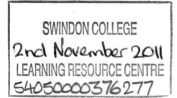

Contents

Preface

There are over 200,000 teaching assistants (TAs) in England alone, working in a whole variety of ways with children of all ages and of all abilities. Until 10 years ago the role of teaching assistants was as diffuse as it was invisible, partly because of the wide variety of tasks they undertook. Now, the value and diversity of tasks that TAs can undertake is recognised and better understood, helped by the recent developments in Workforce Remodelling. In recent years there have also been several government initiatives that impinge upon the work of TAs such as the Every Child Matters agenda, the Children's Plan and the rewrite of the National Curriculum. These changes have necessitated a second edition of this book that aims at unravelling a few of the complexities of school life for new TAs. If you are thinking of becoming a TA or just starting out, reading this book should help you to settle more quickly into what will prove a most fulfilling and interesting career.

TAs used to be seen as an extra pair of hands to wash paint pots and care for grazed knees, then as a useful extra adult to support pupils with special needs. Now, people realise their potential, and teachers and managers use them more effectively. The Literacy and Numeracy strategies of the late 1990s recognised TAs as an important factor in raising standards. TAs help teachers in the crucial areas of teaching and learning with all abilities and ages not just by doing the menial jobs, minding miscreants or supporting the less able. TAs are also a group with an enormous fund of goodwill, enthusiasm and expertise. As their profile has been raised, everyone is more conscious of their role and the need to help a TA to do a good job. Partnership and teamwork have become key issues in schools.

Most TAs have come from a non-academic background and have either been volunteering in school already or wanting a part-time job to fit in with a young family. But, some of you may be graduates thinking of teaching as a career or marking time a little before you go back to a job for which you were trained. Some of you left school several years ago, and want a change of career, and see working with youngsters as more satisfying. That it will be. In all these cases you may think you know how schools work because you went to school, but the changes in the last 10 years have been rapid and significant. Hopefully this book will give you a few pointers to early success and encourage you to learn more about the potential of being a TA.

This book is for TAs who are working in a general capacity in schools, supporting pupils of any ability including those with special educational needs (SEN) or those who are gifted or talented. You will support teachers, and also support the curriculum.

Acknowledgements

I would like to thank:

- all the teaching assistants and teachers who participated in courses and discussions with me over the years. They have been inspirational;

- the young people and staff of William de Ferrers School, Essex for the photographs reused from the first edition;

- Gill Foukes who did the first drafts of the cartoons for the first edition;

- the children and staff of Millfields Primary School, Wivenhoe, Essex for the remaining photographs;

- the Office of Public Sector Information for a licence to use Figure 7.1 from the publication *Independent Review of the Primary Curriculum: Final report* (DCSF 2009b);

- the Local Government Employers for permission to use Table 9.2 from the publication *School Support Staff: The way forward* (NJC 2003);

- Sophie Thomson of Routledge for her speedy and helpful replies to my queries and keeping an eye on me through the writing process; and

- my supportive husband Frank, for his endless patience, general support and his maintenance of my ICT system.

Photographs

Figures

Tables

Abbreviations

AEN	Additional educational needs
AfL	Assessment for learning
APP	Assessing pupils' progress
ASE	Association for Science Education
BIS	Department for Business, Innovation and Skills
CPD	Continuing professional development
CRB	Criminal Records Bureau
CV	curriculum vitae
DATA	Design and Technology Association
DCSF	Department for Children, Schools and Families
DES	Department of Education and Science (does not exist now)
DfEE	Department for Education and Employment
DfES	Department for Education and Skills
DIUS	Department for Innovation, Universities and Skills
DSP	Designated senior person
EAL	English as an additional language
ECM	Every Child Matters
EP	Educational Psychologist
EYFS	Early Years Foundation Stage
FE	Further Education
G&T	Gifted and talented
GCSE	General Certificate of Secondary Education
HLTA	Higher level teaching assistant
HMI	Her Majesty's Inspectorate
ICT	Information and communication technology
IEP	Individual education plan
ISA	Independent Safeguarding Authority
LA	Local Authority
LGA	Local Government Association
LMS	Local management of schools
MRI	Magnetic resonance imaging
NC	National curriculum
NIACE	National Institute for Adult and Continuing Education
NJC	National Joint Council
NOS	National Occupational Standards
NVQ	National Vocational Qualification
Ofsted	Office for Standards in Education, Children's Services and Skills
PE	Physical education
PGCE	Post Graduate Certificate of Education

PSHE	Personal, social and health education
QCA	Qualifications and Curriculum Authority
RAISEonline	Reporting and analysis for improvement through schools self-evaluation
RE	Religious education
SATs	Standardised Assessment Tests or Tasks
SDP/SIP	School Development Plan/School Improvement Plan
SEAL	Social and emotional attitudes to learning
SEF	Self-evaluation form
SEN	Special Educational Needs
SENCO	Special Educational Needs Coordinator
SIP	School Improvement Partner
SoW	Scheme of work
SPACE	Science processes and concept exploration
SRE	Sex and relationship education
SSSNB	School Support Staff Negotiating Body
STI	Standard Tariff Inspection
TA	Teaching assistant
TDA	Training and Development Agency
TTA	Teacher Training Agency
WAMG	Workforce Agreement Monitoring Group

Before you start

IN THE PAST, teaching assistants (TAs) were often appointed in an informal way, such as when the need arose to support a special pupil, or when a bit of extra funding came the way of the school. It is now recognised widely that a TA's post should be properly advertised, with job descriptions and conditions of service available, interviews should be held and the successful candidates should be inducted into becoming a full member of the school staff team. This means that it should be much easier for you to find out beforehand what being a TA will entail. You should also be inducted into and as supported in that post as any other member of staff.

The skills of TAs are not just those of a carer, although that is important. No qualifications are required for the job unless the school stipulates this, but you will need to gain a basic understanding of teaching and learning processes, be part of the whole school team and follow policies and guidelines as set out in school policies as well as being caring and alert. An understanding of the school's context, ethos and philosophy will also help you work better. All this not only helps you to support any children or young people you work with but will also help to raise their expectations, achievements and self-esteem.

The first chapter helps you to think about getting a job as a TA and Chapter 2 gives suggestions for starting off. Chapter 3 emphasises the importance of relationships in affecting all that you do in school. Chapters 4 and 5 examine the principles of learning and teaching in a basic way to get you started on the journey. Given these principles, Chapter 6 looks at the implications of the principles to practise in the classroom. All that happens in a school is its curriculum, largely formal and explicit, some of it legally determined but some of it informal and hidden. Chapter 7 explores this and Chapter 8 looks at the external influences on school life. If you read all this and still want to progress further, Chapter 9 gives you pointers as to the type of career development and professional opportunities there are in being a TA.

You may have various reasons for applying for a job as a TA. The research shows you are likely to be a woman and not a recent school leaver. Only about 3 to 5 per cent of TAs are men, but any men reading this should not be put off by it. Children and young people not only need a male role model but gain immeasurably from the different interests that men can bring to this job. You are probably a parent and have or have had children at school. You may have found the time to go in and help at your children's playgroup, nursery or school. You have found you enjoyed being with your own children, you know a lot about them from having them. As a volunteer, the school staff will have found your help useful. Anyhow, the school has advertised a part-time job, or maybe a member of staff approached you, and you found you could get paid for something you enjoy and that fits in with having the family.

Some of you have recently left school, and think that you may enjoy working with children. In the past, the only possibility of getting qualified to do this was to become a teacher or opt to work with very young children and become a nursery nurse. Many more possibilities, varieties of jobs and directly relevant training are now available and, hopefully, some of you are considering a career as a TA. Some even progress through levels to become qualified teachers, while some qualified teachers opt to be TAs, for they like the ways in which they work. Whatever your background before starting the job, you are bringing a wealth of experience, knowledge and understanding with you. Even if you have a school background, a new job and particularly a different school bring new challenges.

Finding out about the job

There is a little book called *Untold Stories* (O'Brien and Garner 2001) that is a series of accounts of the work of learning support assistants (those who specialise in working with children with special educational need (SEN)). This gives a good flavour of the kind of situations you can find in schools. Circumstances have moved on a lot since it was written but it may help you decide whether this kind of work is for you. Before you apply for any job, make sure you get a job description and find out what the pay and conditions of service are. Ask to walk round the school if you are not already familiar with it. You will get a sense of atmosphere very quickly and could decide that it is or is not a place in which you could spend a lot of time.

You will have to fill in an application form and should have an interview, so you will meet some of the staff before you start, and have visited at least part of the school. Before you start as a new TA, someone in the school should be nominated to take responsibility for your induction (though unfortunately this doesn't always happen). All schools are different, and even if you have done the job before, there are things you need to find out. Chapter 2 will guide you through this

Most TA jobs are for term time only and are part time. Some of you may be among the lucky ones to have found a full-time job although these are still few and far between. The contracts may also only be for distinct pupil contact hours that do not give time for planning, preparation, clearing up and feedback time, all essential to the job. This can be a problem, as many TAs are exploited and expected to do these aspects of the job in their own time. Right from the start you must find out what the expectations of the school are in these areas and clarify for what you are to be paid for. You need to know about how you are going to work in this school. Even if you know the school well, being employed will bring changes. If you are new to the school there should be a six-month probationary period. The expectations of your achievements during this time, the line management structures and times for a review of your progress should be clearly spelt out to you before you agree to accept the post. Termination of a probationary period should not be a surprise to you if you do not perform well – the school must have supported you during that time.

Also, before you start, various checks will be made about you. The school will take up references and will not confirm your appointment until this is satisfactory for them. They will also ask you to complete a form to enable them to make child protection checks about you. If you have already been working in schools or with children this may be easy, as a national database is being prepared into which the school may be able to link. Until very recently all people working in any capacity with children had to undergo checks with the Criminal Records Bureau (CRB) in any new establishment they joined. The new Independent Safeguarding Authority (ISA) has been set up to streamline this necessary, but cumbersome, procedure. Health checks are rare these days.

Becoming a professional

Think carefully before applying. Undertaking paid employment means you are responsible for things such as attendance, punctuality and carrying out your job to the best of your ability.

Also, working with children and young people, in a team of professionals, means that you are going to take a responsible role in the lives of other people, particularly young people, and thus with the more vulnerable members of our society. You will be aiming to become a professional, in the wider sense of that term, yourself. It is not something to undertake lightly. You may have to rearrange things at home. Child care of your own children, before and/or after school, may be needed if you are to talk to teachers out of pupil contact time, and attend meetings and courses. You should be prepared to undertake some form of continuing professional development CPD, however slight. Child care may be needed if your children are ill, although usually senior staff are understanding, so long as you do not take advantage of them. You may need to rearrange your domestic routines to fit in with the new job. It really helps if partners or family members understand what your new commitments might entail, and if friends understand you are not as free to do the things you may have been used to doing. But be sure to leave time for yourself and your family; you do not want to gain a job but lose something else you value. Being a rounded person with outside activities and responsibilities means you are a more interesting individual to be with the pupils.

Beware of taking on too much. Becoming a midday assistant as well as a teaching assistant may seem to make sense in terms of continuity for the pupils, but it can mean you do not get your lunch until after school. Snacking or omitting meals does not help your body. A break from work, even for a short time, refreshes your mind and is legally required.

Your development

Beginning a new job or career is a good time to take stock. You nay have made all the decisions before reading this book, but either way, just take a few moments to consider yourself.

Questions to ask yourself:

- Why do I want to take up paid employment with all the responsibilities that will come with being an employee?

- Why do I want to work with children or young people?

- Why do I want to work in a school rather than be a childminder or a nurse?

- What do I value in my life? Take time to think about this one:

  My home, family, friends, money, material goods, looking good, helping people, being someone, my place of worship, my interests, having time to myself . . .?

- Are any of these values likely to come into conflict with those of other people or an institution?

If you have given time to these questions, decisions about how, when and where you work will be easier. Answering questions in an interview will be easier because you are sure of yourself, who you are and where you want to go in your life. The answers are not once and for ever – you may change, events may change you, but taking up work with children deserves a lot of consideration.

You will have a responsibility to your school as an employee, to the children in your charge, to the teacher you work with, but you also have responsibilities to yourself and your family. Before starting your job you should have worked out how you are going to cope with your other commitments such as child care, looking after the house, shopping and any other family responsibilities that you have. You will have planned your day and week but do take a moment to consider emergencies.

Work out what you are going to do if:

- your children are ill;

- any other member of your family falls ill or has severe personal needs;

- your means of transport on which you depend to get to school lets you down;

- any of your home equipment fails – fridge or washing machine – and needs servicing.

Everyone needs to consider their own personal and professional development whether or not they are in paid employment. Becoming a TA is an indicator that you are interested in the development of children and young people. All of us are learners and continue learning throughout our lives. Hopefully the school you have joined or are considering joining is a learning community where all the adults as well as the pupils associated with it are learners and are operating as a whole school team. Thinking of or starting a new job is a very good place to take stock of yourself and think about where you want to be in the future. This is often an interview question.

One way of organising your thoughts positively before an interview – you will have to complete an application form anyway – is to review your achievements to date. All of us have certain documents we need to keep for a lifetime, beginning with a birth certificate. It is very useful to have some sort of record of your education, your experiences, both within and outside work, and somewhere to keep those documents so that you know where they are when life

FIGURE 1.1 Making a start on yourself

sends you new opportunities. This kind of organisation of your paperwork makes completing forms or compiling a curriculum vitae (CV) much easier. You will have a wealth of experiences that are not documented but that are worth recognising as your individual potential. Doing a review does a great deal for your self-esteem if you ever feel a little low.

Keeping a portfolio

You could consider starting a personal professional development portfolio. This is really just a loose-leaf collection of information and evidence about you. You could start one even before you start a job, as you will have to find some of the information for the application form. Some schools have a system and may offer help in this but start your own portfolio to keep at home. Any ringbinder will do, but the larger ones are best for this. Think of your personal portfolio as a reference collection, and have other files or folders for working documents, such as course notes or school policies when you start getting those.

Keeping a record of your personal and professional development

Have dividers in your ringbinder for:

- your personal information and history;

- your place of work and relevant documents;

- your job and how it is going;

- documentation concerning any professional development review or appraisals that you may have;

- your own notes;

- a record of the course details, dates and outcomes of courses, any associated certificates that you want to keep for reference later;

- letters of appreciation or references.

The thin plastic pockets designed for ringfiles are ideal containers for documents such as certificates, but you will need extra wide dividers if you use these.

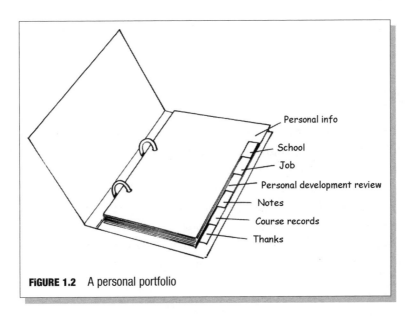

FiGURE 1.2 A personal portfolio

The first or personal section

You have a wealth of life experiences regardless of formal qualifications. Don't underestimate these or undervalue yourself. Some of them you may have forgotten about until you do this task. For instance, you may have learnt a language to go on holiday, which could be really helpful later. Parenting skills are useful for a TA, as are the organisation skills that you might have developed in connection with running a home or social activities. Being an officer in a sports club and your practical 'do-it-yourself' skills are all useful achievements. Sewing, cooking, potting, painting and other practical skills are taught in today's schools. Caring skills, first aid experience and organising skills from running things like scouts or guides, coaching sport, all can be useful, whatever age the pupils.

The pages could be:

Personal details:

- your name, address, telephone number etc.;

- a note of all those important numbers that you can never find: National Insurance number, hospital number, car registration, telephone number of next of kin and your solicitor, and so on.

Your educational history:

- the names of schools and colleges you have been to and dates attended;

- what examinations you have taken and what the results were;

- any other courses you have taken and what qualifications you have gained, with grades and dates (keep any certificates and diplomas here).

Life experiences:

- what things you have done other than paid employment: parenting, caring, clubs and societies, craft and domestic achievements, interests, sports and hobbies.

Employment experiences with dates:

- record anything you have produced: a booklet, a craft object, even a child! (you could keep photos of them here).

Anything else that might be relevant that you want to keep a record of:

- holidays/travel experiences, disasters you coped with, major events you attended.

Other things to think of

Being a TA can be emotionally demanding. The circumstances of some pupils may distress you. You will become close to some pupils, particularly if you are to assist one with special needs. As a professional you will need to be more objective than a parent, yet properly caring. This is why it is important to have someone in the school to share your feelings with. All school staff need personal support in their job at some time, so do not be afraid to ask what the arrangements are for staff support and guidance. Also, it will be important to retain confidentiality about these matters, as they will not be ones to share outside the school. Cosy, gossipy chats about such matters over a cup of coffee or a pint will not be possible, so do consider this.

While there are no formal qualification requirements for TAs, the work you will do even with those in pre-school settings, will have considerable emphasis on a basic understanding of English and mathematics. You do need to be fairly literate and numerate yourself. Accurate spoken English is not easy for some, brought up in areas where the dialect is ungrammatical, or with English as your second language, but with the emphasis on speaking and listening these days, it does need consideration. Talk to someone in the school if you are concerned about any of these areas. Your alternative language may be just what they are looking for.

Also, it is not possible to be a TA in a school these days without basic information and communication technology (ICT) skills. Access to your own computer would also be a great asset. Much school documentation is kept electronically, many schools communicate with staff and parents electronically and government documents are often only downloadable rather than provided in hard copy. Also, all children from the early years are expected to use computers, classrooms will have interactive whiteboards connected to the internet and school networks that you will be expected to use or at least be familiar with.

Take it one step at a time. In this way you will gain confidence, and knowledge and understanding. Having a social life, reading novels, listening to music or doing whatever interests you, is essential to keeping you a balanced and interesting person. You can then bring to the staffroom or the classroom another dimension or opinion. You may find you want to take artefacts (objects of interest) into school from home, or collect home things to use in school, such as photographs or things you find on holiday. It sometimes becomes difficult to separate school life from home life, and this is a balance that you have to find for yourself.

If you are going to study at all at home, even reading a bit here and there, find a space on the shelves for your school things and try to find a time just for you. Some TAs, studying for the longer courses, end up working after everyone else in the house has gone to bed. This may work for a short time, but it should not become a lifestyle. Do talk these sorts of things over with your family members; they may have ideas to help, and it is good to involve them in preparing for your new experiences.

Being professional also means that, even if you are concerned about things at home, once you step over the threshold of the school you give school matters your full attention. Smile, and respond to others. Remember, we all have problems – and putting them aside for a time may even help us cope with them. If it is really difficult, you will be able to find your line manager and talk it through at a convenient time for you both.

Maybe becoming a TA should carry a health warning – beware enthusiasm! Once you start, you will want to learn more, take more courses, become a better TA; you may even want to go on to get a degree if you do not have one, become a teacher or a senior TA. You do not have to do it all at once. It may be that you need a year or so out of your career as a TA to undertake some family commitment, to care for a sick relative, or because your partner's job or own children's needs become more demanding. Do not worry about it; nothing you do in the job or at home is wasted, it all adds up to the person that is you. Once you apply and are successful, enjoy the job. Being a TA is a very satisfying career, never dull, and full of opportunity.

Getting started in the job

UNIT
4

MUCH WAS LEARNT by new TAs in the past by osmosis, just watching and listening to what the teachers do and imitating them. While this is useful, it is important that you understand the reasons for what you do, most particularly that you know what the learning intentions of the teachers are. It is important that you work under the direction of qualified teachers at all times. Teachers carry responsibility for the learning of the pupils in their class, and for this responsibility, teachers have a long training and different pay scales from TAs.

Hopefully, when you take up the post you will be able to enlist the help of a friendly teacher in the school, usually called a mentor, who will help you through your first year – an induction year. You can do this formally, through your line manager or your head teacher, or informally. However, you do need to remember that teachers these days are under considerable pressure to do many things outside their pupil contact hours, and may not feel they have the time to undertake mentoring a TA. But those who have agreed to do it have gained in the long run from having a more informed assistant, one who understands the context of the classrooms and schools in which he or she works. If you undertake the Local Authority (LA) induction course, which is based on nationally produced and highly recommended materials, you will need a mentor anyway.

Questions to ask yourself as you start:

- To whom can you turn in your school to act as a mentor while you read this book?

- What kind of induction will you get?

- What is the process for reviewing your progress in your probationary period?

- With whom can you discuss issues outside the school, bearing in mind confidentiality?

- Where might you find further reading or study materials in your locality?

- Who can tell you about local courses and qualifications and whether you can get financial help or advise you on career and professional development?

- What does the LA in your area provide? Where are the local colleges?

- To whom would you go if you had a personal problem?

The DCFS (Department for Children, Families and Schools) has produced a comprehensive induction training course that all LAs deliver. Basically it covers four days away from the school and is best attended during your first year working in a school. Some authorities also have additional days with specialist subjects. Each student gets a file of materials that are covered in the course. Do ask about whether you can go on this, in your area. You may have to go in your own time but the course itself is free.

Before you start

Get your map of the classrooms, and put a name to each area. Then, if you have an accident in any of them, want to know anything about the area, or would like to borrow something from them, you will know to whom to go. School buildings are confusing. Changes in the way pupils are taught have brought changes to the use of areas. More class teaching means some schools have put up walls in previously open-plan areas. The developments of ICT have meant computer suites becoming as common as libraries. You need to know the school layout. Classes are not necessarily organised in year groups, or even in Key Stages. It depends on the numbers of children in the school, the accommodation and the management decisions of the school.

You will need to know:

- your way about (maybe there is a map?);

- where to hang your coat and where the toilet facilities are;

- what to wear – some schools have a 'dress code' for every day; some lessons such as science need protective clothing, while others such as PE need special clothing, especially appropriate footware;

- when and where to go for a refreshment break or lunch and where you should spend any non-contact time taken in school – staffroom or?

- what the protocols are on using school equipment – from the telephone to the photocopier, provision of pencils and paper, etc. for your use;

- who to go to for any information about your job;

- what to do if you are ill on the premises or cannot come to work;

- how the school can contact you in the event of a school closure, say in bad weather or a burst boiler;

- what the guidelines are about pupils' and adults' behaviour, and what the pupils are to call you;

- when your job description will be reviewed, and how;

- who will brief you about child protection and confidentiality;

- what is expected of you regarding attendance at meetings and going on courses;.

- what are the communication systems for policies, dates, changes;

- what access do you have to school documentation – is there a school handbook for you?

Some of this may seem obvious, but can frequently be overlooked. Assumptions can be made by busy managers that you know all this kind of thing.

You do need to know some of the school's policies, particularly those on Health and Safety, Confidentiality and Child Protection, right from the start. There is more detail about these in the next chapter. Many schools now have a staff handbook, and some even have one especially for TAs. Handbooks usually contain valuable information about life in the school in general, who does what and when, and who is responsible for each subject, area, and resource that you might need. It will give you names of governors, and titles and locations of policies to which you might want to refer.

Once you have established to whom you go to about your job, you can then work with them to find out all the other matters. You will be working directly with a qualified teacher who is responsible for your work as well as that of all the pupils in the class. Sometimes, indeed, teachers have felt that TAs are an added burden, like an extra pupil. It is up to you to prove them wrong! You will also be responsible to a line manager such as the SENCO (the co-ordinator of children with SEN), a subject head or possibly a deputy head or head teacher. You will be working in a classroom with one or more pupils.

You will become a professional, a member of staff, even if you are employed for only five hours a week. This gives you a status with the pupils. You may have worked in the local playgroup before you came to the job, where they called you by your first name, and treated you as an auntie. The pupils in the school will see you differently, and this helps you to be firm about school matters, and yet maintain the friendly approach. Calling pupils by their first names and being called by your family name, with an appropriate title – Mr, Mrs or Miss – establishes your position, particularly if you are near to the pupils in age, or knew them more informally before becoming a TA. This does not mean you are distant or pompous, just professional. Mutual respect is the foundation for good relationships. Being appropriately friendly, establishing rapport and the foundations for a working relationship with both staff and pupils are important. The reasons for this will become clearer as you read on.

Responsibility

Even with the introduction of higher level TAs (HLTAs), the regulations for using support staff to relieve the teachers' workload (DfES 2003a) indicate that, whatever level you are working at, there will still be supervision of your work, whatever you are asked to do. Ultimate responsibility for teaching and learning of pupils will be with the qualified teacher. You may have academic qualifications that are better than the teacher you work with but your pay and conditions of service will depend on your contract.

You should have been given a job description when you started, and so it should be clear to you what you have to do. In the beginning it is unlikely that you will have too many different things to do, but the nature of the job is to support and assist where you can. If you have particular responsibilities these should be clearly laid out for you. As you get settled, you may be asked to do something different, or work in a different place, with different people. Or you may begin to offer to do other things. Keep a note of these so that when your job description is reviewed (which it should be, at least annually) you can have the new tasks written into a revised version. Your professional portfolio would be a good place for any notes you want to keep. There are many examples of job descriptions published now: see the *Good Practice Guide* (DfES 2000: 18) and TDA (Training and Development Agency) induction materials (TDA 2006a, 2006b: 2.13).

The job description will also detail to whom you are responsible and should include a date for review. You will have a line manager who may or may not be the class teacher with whom you work most closely.

Ground rules

The main problems, if there are any, seem to lie with communication and relationships. Do ask questions if you are not sure. In the past, so often TAs were expected to understand what to do or where to go by a process of osmosis. You had to observe your teacher, use your innate intelligence and guess what to do. Teachers are rarely trained to manage people even now, only to manage learning or manage pupils, so you can help them be explicit by questioning them. Don't think they might be too busy. It is in the children's best interest that you know what to do and why, and the teacher knows your strengths or limitations. Your arrival in a classroom should not give rise to extra problems for the teacher or the pupils, so clarify things from the start. Discuss the following list of useful ground rules with each of the teachers with whom you are going to work. You may find that just talking the list through with them will be enough, but it is wise to check that you don't need to do anything more formal. If in doubt or you come across any difficulties, discuss them with your line manager.

Useful ground rules

Before you start in the classroom find out:

- where to go in the room, or whether you are to work outside the room;

- if outside, where you go for help and when you are to complete your time with the pupils;

- whether you can approach the teacher during the lesson;

- what decisions you can make for yourself;

- when you can talk things over with the teacher;

- where you can find materials to work with;

- which pupils you are going to work with and what their particular needs are;

- what you are to do with them and why – what is the purpose of their task?

Find out:

- what kind of end product the teacher expects, or is it the doing of the task that is important (or both);

- what do you do if a pupil asks to go to the toilet;

- what to do if the pupils misbehave or things go wrong;

- what to do if they finish what the teacher wanted them to do;

- whether you can write in their books or on their worksheets;

- how the teacher wants to hear about how the pupils did the task;

- whether you contribute or question during the teacher's input time;

- whether you are able to communicate anything about the pupil with their parents or carers;

- whether you will be expected to attend any meetings regarding the pupils you will be working with – such as parents' evenings or SEN reviews;

- whether you can tidy the rooms, the desks or the resources areas;

- what the expectations are regarding the pupils clearing up;

- if there is anything the teacher wants you to avoid doing.

You need to establish lines of communication with the teacher of that class before you go there for the first time. Do not arrive at a classroom after the lesson has started unless you have spoken to the teacher first.

Establish some lines of communication for the future to ensure that you:

- understand the needs of the pupils with whom you are to work;

- know how to find out what the teacher wants you to do on a regular basis;

- know what the pupils are expected to learn and achieve in the time you are with them;

- know what sorts of things you can do or plan to do on your own initiative.

As you get to know your way around the school and the classroom, try hard to remember names. Watch how other members of staff do things, and talk this over with your mentor or line manager if you are seeing different practices in different places. You need to establish what the senior management are aiming for, as well as what the individual teachers want.

You may find it useful to make yourself a kit that you carry with you. This could be in a sturdy shopping bag or a small plastic carrier box.

A TA kit could consist of:

- spare pencils and pens, rubbers and a good pencil sharpener with a reservoir for sharpenings;

- a ruler;

- a notepad or exercise book for personal jottings;

- a pad of 'post-its';

- a box of tissues or a toilet roll (for runny noses);

- spare clean A4 plain and lined paper;

- scrap paper;

- scissors for you and the pupils;

- Blu Tack and Sellotape®;

- a few paper towels (for spillages);

- a dictionary.

You would then add anything relevant to what you are going to do:

- a few reference books or pictures related to the topic;

- spare parts or batteries or a screwdriver or crayons;

- artefacts related to the topic – stones, models . . .;

- mathematical apparatus or a calculator;

- measuring equipment – a stopwatch or datalogger;

- goggles for science and DT.

Duty of care

You have a duty of care whenever you are working with people, but most particularly when you're working with children. For some of you, this may be your main task. If you are appointed to work with a physically disabled child for a particular task or have a post in a special school as a care assistant, care may be your main duty. If that is the case then you will need specialist guidance and training for the particular skills you need. Start by talking with the SENCO to find out what support and training is available locally. This book doesn't aim to cover special needs but there are plenty of books that do. A good place to start is the Routledge David Fulton Publishers' special needs list. Check their website www.routledge.com for some ideas. Your SENCO may have copies of some of them already.

Whatever children you are working with you must be very clear about the school policies for dealing with behaviour and child protection; there is more about both of these in the next chapter. The government has tightened up procedures and training opportunities in both these areas in the last few years, indeed after a high profile case concerning a little girl, Victoria Climbié, the whole system from Ofsted through local authorities to the school itself has had to respond to a new framework. The initial Green paper was entitled *Every Child Matters* (ECM) (DfES 2004a). Subsequent documentation and changes refer to the ECM agenda. The five outcomes towards which these changes are aimed are worth remembering as they are now regarded to be what we must all aim to achieve with children. They are about care in the widest sense:

1 **Being healthy:** Children should enjoy good mental and physical health and living a healthy lifestyle.

2 **Staying safe:** They must be protected from harm and neglect.

3 **Enjoying and achieving:** They should be getting the most out of life and developing the skills of adulthood.

4 **Making a positive contribution:** They should be involved with the community and society and not engaging in antisocial or offending behaviour.

5 **Economic well-being:** They should not be prevented by economic disadvantage from achieving their full potential in life.

Your workplace information

If you have completed any form of induction you will already have gained some pieces of information about your school. You may have been given a copy of a school file with useful information. If you have started a personal professional portfolio, now is the time to make a start on the second section – details about your job.

This section can begin with your job description. You could also include any notes regarding your employment: your contract, information about your employer, discipline and grievance procedures, performance review procedures and so on. There will be other less technical information that it is useful to find out and retain.

In the TDA induction file there is a really useful checklist of things to find out about your school (TDA 2006a, 2006b: 2.2–2.7). It covers the following areas:

1 Do you know the key facts about your school setting?

This includes items about numbers of pupils, teachers and support staff and key stages, any specialisms or defining characteristics of the school.

2 Do you know about the local community?

This includes items about the locality itself and who makes up the community, employment patterns and community activities.

3 Do you know what the governing body does and who the governors are?

4 What regular visitors from the local authority, other services, agencies or teams come to the school?

This includes what contact the TA may have with such people.

5 How is the school organised?

This includes class groupings, guidance on systems and procedures, policies, resources, internet access, etc.

6 Are you familiar with school procedures?

This refers to a school handbook and procedure on health and safety, confidentiality and child protection, security, expectations of behaviour management.

7 How does the school provide for pupils' differing needs?

This is about access to the *Code of Practice* for SEN, and resources and people who can support SEN or pupils with EAL (English as an additional language).

8 What do you know about the curriculum?

This asks about familiarity with key stage demands of the NC, the strategies, assessment procedures and inclusion implications, the SDP/SIP (school development/improvement plan) and accountability strategies including inspection.

9 What is your school/LA doing in relation to the ECM agenda?

This asks questions about each of the five areas.

10 What training and development opportunities are available in your school/setting or local area?

The secondary induction includes a separate section asking 'What do you know about qualifications?' (This is referring to the qualifications the school offers pupils not what is available to the TAs.)

Some of this will be useful to you when you read the next chapter. If you get any addresses, policies or other information about the school, the file will be a useful place to keep it, then you will know where to put your hands on it. The next chapter on the school context has suggestions of policies that you should know about. You may collect too much paper here but you could put a reference to what they are and where you can find them in the file instead. You may not need full copies of everything – just a reference or a photocopy of the relevant pages may be enough. If you are given a school handbook, it should contain all this information.

Yourself and your job

Be wary of talking about people or pupils you meet in your new job. It is tempting to tell someone about incidents that occur or personal details about people that you learn from conversations, but being a professional means sharing comments of that nature only with your professional colleagues. Confidentiality about school matters is vital. However, you can and should talk about the principles of the job outside the school. Talking always helps you clear your mind, and putting thoughts into words means you have to organise those thoughts. Don't bore your family though!

It is important when working in schools to recognise that you too are a learner. Schools are a learning community. This means keeping your eyes and ears open all the time, asking questions if you do not understand and being prepared to read more about anything that interests you. Make notes of things that interest you but always keep names out of any account. At whatever level you enter, whatever your expectations for the future, this is not a repetitive job. No two days are the same nor are any two children even identical twins. You are aiming to be what is called a 'reflective practitioner', thinking and reflecting about what you do and always looking to do it better. This gives you job satisfaction as well as improving standards for the pupils.

Performance reviews

Different schools have different ways of helping their staff progress and monitoring their work. You will have a six-month probationary period during which there should be several formal, but most likely short, meetings with your line manager to reassure both of you that your work is both satisfying to you and satisfactory to the school. If things are going wrong, any termination of this period should not come as a surprise at the end because of these reviews. More positively, they give everybody opportunities to improve things as you go along. Then, yearly, all employees should have an opportunity for a review of their work with a more senior professional and an opportunity to consider future developments. The last chapter looks at performance reviews in more detail. You file would be a good place to keep any paperwork associated with such a process. Some organisations have more informal one-to-one reviews more frequently than once a year, maybe only a phone conversation or brief chat over a cup of tea – again you can just note the date and outcome here.

Other sections in the portfolio

The rest of the file will become more useful as you progress in your job, but it will be a place where you can keep your notes until their value becomes clearer to you. You should also keep a record of any meetings or courses you go to, adding where you can what use these may have been to you. If you go on a course, you will probably get handouts, you may have to write essays, or do observations. These will be bulky so you will need a separate file or wallet for the course materials. Keep your thank-you letters, or comments on your work as a TA from visitors. They are lovely to look back on if you start wondering why you do what you do or get a bit low. You might keep photographs of visits or activities with which you have been involved, programmes of school productions, cuttings from the local paper recording events in the school. It is somewhere to keep notes of your own thoughts about your job for future reference if they do not need immediate action.

The aim of all this paper collection is to be able to reflect on your job and your achievements so that you can improve your personal competence, and maintain your own self-esteem and self-confidence.

Find out

- Is there a local group you can join to discuss ideas with?

- Do you know about the practices of and around TAs in other schools?

- What do you know about national initiatives and associations that could support you in your job?

Being part of the school team

Relationships matter

Your school

SCHOOLS ARE COMPLEX PLACES. Not only will they have a number of adult employees, which means they range from a small to a very large business, they will also have pupils for whom they are responsible who can number from twenty plus in a small rural school to over 3,000 in a large sixth form college. Not only do these pupils have to be educated, they are not adults and so the school is responsible for their safety. There are many government directives and initiatives, local influences and parental wishes, all to be considered. No two schools are alike, even in similar localities with similar intakes and buildings. People make the difference. Schools are organic, living, always changing.

Think about the following list of characteristics of an effective school. It was drawn up after a large research project in some London schools called *School Matters* (Mortimore *et al.* 1988). The project identified some key characteristics of successful schools, which were:

- leadership – staff selection, consensus and unity of purpose, professionalism and understanding;

- shared vision and goals;

- attractive and orderly environment with self-managing classrooms, reflecting positive ethos;

- concentration on teaching and learning – monitoring of effective time spent;

- purposeful, well-organised teaching, clear pace, structure, and objectives reflected in preparation, effective questioning strategies;

- high expectations and self-esteem of teachers, pupils and parents;

- positive reinforcement, clear feedback, rewards and disciplinary procedures;

- monitoring of progress, focusing on goals, informing planning and teaching;

- pupil rights and responsibilities enabling pupil participation, raising self-esteem and independent learning;

- home–school partnerships fostering support and making demands;

- senior managers and teachers, as well as students continue to be learners.

(Sammons and Mortimore 1995)

Can you see how you can be part of such a school? Another similar list that you can discuss with your mentor or line manager is derived from the principles of the International School Effectiveness and Improvement Centre. They are that:

- all children can learn, albeit in different ways at different rates;

- individual schools can make a substantial difference to the development, progress and achievement of pupils;

- effective schools add value to pupils' lives;

- effective schools focus on a range of learning outcomes, including academic, practical, creative, personal and social;

- schools improve most by focusing on learning and teaching, while also addressing their culture and internal conditions;

- partnership is a fundamental element of successful school improvement;

- intervention work needs to be based on appropriate research findings.

(Sammons 1999: 340)

Teams

TAs are part of the classroom partnership, the TA team, the support staff and the whole school team. School policies affect you and you should be included in all the appraisal or performance management strategies, pay, grievance and discipline policies, and in all the staff training relevant to the pupils or curriculum with which you are involved. Having rights always brings with it responsibilities, so you must be prepared to play your part as a member of the team. You may be employed on a part-time basis but nowadays part-timers have equal opportunities for pensions (superannuation), sick pay and holidays with respect to the time they work. Many teachers work part time too.

In order to play your part in the team and feel supported by the organisation and the rest of the staff you need to understand something of the way in which schools work, and to keep yourself up to date and contribute where you can. Most of what is written in this chapter refers to state schools. Independent schools may well have different ways of organising themselves. The school building will have little effect on the structure and systems, which are how the school works. Many schools still operate very effectively in old buildings; there are open plan schools where walls have been built and Victorian buildings where walls have been knocked down; some schools are opened in purpose built, environmentally friendly buildings but still have problems. All have their joys and drawbacks. What makes a school an effective and pleasant place to be in are the people who work in the building. This chapter will look more closely at the organisation within the building and the ways in which people operate.

Getting to know who is who

You will have met several teachers, have a designated line manager, and have identified the SENCO – sometimes called the inclusion manager. The head teacher may or may not have been part of your appointment process, but you should be aware who that person is. If you do not have a copy of a staff file you could try to complete the checklist in the box. You may need help, and you will not be able to do it all at once.

As you ask, you will begin to find out what those jobs involve, and how they affect you. It is useful to make contact with the caretaker early on, so that when you want help with spilt paint, need bin bags, or find a leak, you know whom to contact. You also need to identify the people responsible for the curriculum areas in which you will be working so that you know how to get resources and answers to your questions.

Who does what in your school?

Photocopy this sheet and add in the names on it.

(The same names may appear in many different boxes if your school is small, as people have to double up on the jobs.)

TABLE 3.1 Responsibilities within your school

Responsibility	Teacher	Governor	Other adult
Head teacher			
Deputy/assistant head(s)			
English			
Mathematics			
Science			
ICT			
Other subjects with which you might be connected:			
Children with SEN – the SENCO			
Assessment or examinations			
Health and Safety			
Child protection issues – the designated senior person (DSP)			
First aid			
Your line management			
Staff professional development			
Finance officer			
Liaison with other schools			
Liaison with outside agencies			
The office manager			
The cleaning			
The site management (caretaker)			
The kitchen			
The grounds			
Other:			

The Essential Guide for New Teaching Assistants, 2nd edn, Routledge © Anne Watkinson 2010

Relationships

It is all very well listing names and finding out roles but the real core of whether any organisation works well depends on the relationships of the people within the organisation. If people get on well together, they will enjoy their work and put much more into it. The wheels of the systems are oiled and run smoothly when people respect each other, remember simple things such as good manners, share ideas and resources and are prepared to step outside the strict description of their job role. In schools, this respect and all that goes with it also applies to the way in which the adults treat the pupils. The aim is for the pupils to treat each other and the adults in the same way. They certainly won't if the adults are falling out with each other! The staff need to work together and will make various teams. There may be a TA team to which you will belong, but you may also be part of a year group team or a subject-oriented team. It may be a team formed briefly to work out a plan for producing the pantomime or to discuss a particular problem or child.

You will certainly need to think of your relationship with the teachers you will be working with. This needs to develop into a partnership. This is more difficult in secondary schools because you are much more likely to be in many different lessons. Nevertheless, you need to make an effort to get to know those teachers outside the classroom. Introduce yourself in the staffroom. Ask those questions about how the teacher wants to work with you, find ways of communicating before and after a lesson. Talk with whoever is your line manager, possibly the SENCO, about the need to get to know the various teachers so that they know your name and role.

In primary schools, many schools have allocated a TA to a specific teacher and it is much easier to get a working relationship going quickly. This may well turn into a 'critical friendship' eventually where you complement each other's way of working and can discuss methods and children's needs easily with each other. You work as a team in the classroom.

PHOTOGRAPH 3.1　A teacher, a TA and a SENCO discussing a particular problem

PHOTOGRAPH 3.2   Partnership in practice

Governance

A school is not only made up of staff and pupils – parents and governors have roles to play. These people are sometimes called stakeholders. Governors usually have a rota for visiting the school so that they can get to know it. If they have the responsibility for the school, they have to know how it looks and works on a day-to-day basis. Do talk with your teacher/mentor about the governing body in your school, who is on it and why, and see what interests they have in the locality. Staff have representation on the governing body, and all related paperwork, except the most confidential items, is available for the public to read.

Your school has a name, which will give some indication of how it is governed or run. It might be a church school and these can be run differently. The status of the school affects the way it is funded, which in turn may affect how and what you are paid. All state or maintained schools have to follow the national curriculum (NC). *Foundation* schools are the employers and the governing body owns the buildings and are responsible for running the school. They may use the LA payroll facilities or an independent firm. In *community* and *voluntary controlled* schools the LA is the employer, and usually the paymaster: that is, they send out the pay cheques. However, a charity or faith will own the buildings of a controlled school and have members of the named faith on their governing body. In a *voluntary aided* school the buildings are owned by the faith or charity, which will also part fund the school. Here the governors are also the employers, as in a foundation school. If your school is a secondary school it may or may not have a sixth form. It could be an academy or a trust school where industry or business partly finance the school, and may have representatives on the governing body. It is likely to be a specialist school in some area of the curriculum, where extra money has gone into resources for that curriculum area. Do ask if you are interested in the governance side of things.

The School Development Plan

One key document of a school, is the SDP/SIP (School Development Plan/School Improvement Plan), as its main intention is to ensure all the 'stakeholders' know what the school is aiming to do. They can also develop systems to create change for the better. The SDP is the business plan for the organisation called school. It should have strategic and long-term ideas of where the school wants to be in 2 or 3 years' time, and a more detailed plan of what is going to happen in the year ahead. It will take into account the aims of the school, and the vision of the governors for the school. It has to take account of any legally imposed or recommended national initiatives. It will have looked at the strengths and weaknesses of the school, in order to consider what changes need to be made, and what can be built on. It sets out the costs of the improvements for the year, and who will be responsible for them, so it should include something about the role of TAs.

Thus, some of the changes planned will affect you. Ask your mentor to show you any relevant bits. Since staff are included in the plan, they should also be consulted about how well last year's plan worked for them, and what could be included for the future as well as know what their role is in the coming year. It is your responsibility to be as well informed as you can be, if you want to play a part in these team consultations. As you feel confident you should also take part in any consultation exercise.

Structure

Just as you are responsible to a line manager, so each person is responsible to someone 'above' them. The school staff structure can look like a pyramid with the head teacher at the top or may have a flatter management structure. The senior management team may consist entirely of senior teachers or may include senior support staff such as the finance officer or bursar, or a senior TA or the site manager. The head teacher has responsibility for running the school, but that responsibility is only delegated to the head by the governing body. They are responsible for what goes on in the school. It is worth finding out governors' names (they may have their photographs in the foyer) and having a look at some of their documentation. Governors do not have responsibilities in the same way as staff, as they have to act as a body, but they will have separate specialities such as for SEN or science. They are responsible for the strategic direction of the schools and for monitoring – they are accountable for the standards, the funds, the building and the appointment of staff – the 'buck' stops with them. They usually have separate committees to discuss things about the school such as finances or premises. Support staff, as part of the whole staff, are able to elect representatives to the governing body, the number depending on the size of the school. The staff representatives should know where minutes of meetings of the governing body are kept, and what the governors' views are of the TAs in your school. You could add this person's name to your checklist box.

The head may or may not have an official deputy, but someone will be appointed to deputise in their absence. This person would then take responsibility for the day-to-day running, and be in charge in a case of emergency. You should know who this person is. Communication systems vary in schools. Some have various forms of daily and weekly diaries. There may be a noticeboard in the staffroom to ensure this communication works. Many schools now, especially secondary ones, communicate electronically. All teaching staff will have laptops and usually there is stand-alone computer in the staffroom for any member of staff to use. Some schools have assistant heads who have particular responsibilities other than deputising for the head, such as inclusion or key stage coordination.

Your line manager may or may not be part of a senior manager team. In secondary schools, the subject leaders are called departmental heads. Some staff take cross-curricular leadership roles, as year group or key stage leader, and they may lead in planning and assessment strategies for a group of teachers. You may be slotted into any one of these managerial teams. They often have their own systems and structures, meetings and resources areas. Teachers in larger schools get extra salary points for teaching and learning responsibility, but in smaller schools these points are correspondingly fewer. Ask about it. Extra responsibility may involve a pastoral role such as looking after staff development, pupil care, parent liaison or SEN; it is unlikely to be for organisational matters such as timetabling, display, an environmental area or the library as the pay must be linked to teaching and learning. Sometimes, some of these latter responsibilities may be taken on by TAs. TAs can be assistant SENCOs but the SENCO must be a qualified teacher. Other salary points for teachers may be for their advanced skills for which they have to be an exemplar both in their own schools and for neighbouring schools. There is more about pay for TAs in the last chapter.

In schools for children of 11 and older, teachers may have a pastoral or tutorial responsibility for a year group class, but will have been appointed for their subject expertise. All teachers now have to have a degree in a NC subject. The plan is that in secondary schools you teach those subjects in which you have most expertise. Unfortunately, it does not always work like that, and there are mismatches. Some subjects are less popular than others. Modern languages and religious education (RE) teachers are scarce, as are mathematics and physics teachers. Teachers no longer have to cover for absent colleagues over a certain number of hours a week. They may, however, have to teach a different subject to the one they qualified in – a biologist may teach physics for instance. Teachers in secondary schools are directed to teach their specialist subjects across several age ranges, and so teach many more children, often up to 200 a week. Primary teachers usually have a class that they teach for most subjects, and children spend most of the day with the one adult. This makes a significant difference to the way in which you operate. A very few authorities have middle schools where there will be some discrete subject teaching with specialised areas such as laboratories or gymnasia and some more general class teaching as in primary schools.

Visitors

Local people from the surrounding community can get involved in the life of the school. They may contribute to the resources. Some businesses may visit or even exchange staff, or they may encourage visits to their premises. Other local services such as the police or the health service may have representatives who make regular visits to the school. The priest, vicar, minister, rabbi, imam or other religious people may be seen at assembly or in the classrooms of any school, not just those with a religious title in their name. Some schools visit their local place of worship regularly and others never go near. All these contacts add a dimension to the school.

You may have been a parent working as a volunteer before becoming a TA. There will possibly be a number of volunteers working in the school. Parents are often consulted on matters such as school uniform, or the best way of relaying news of a pupil's progress. They run associations, usually to raise money for the school. As a TA you may be asked to liaise with particular parents about their children who have special needs, but usually the teacher deals directly with them on all curriculum matters. Be careful not to be drawn in by parents who ask you about their child's progress or behaviour at school. Refer them to the teacher concerned. You may be asked to join the teacher or the SENCO when reviews take place of pupils with SEN, particularly if you are closely associated with that pupil. The teacher concerned will advise you about your role in that meeting.

At some time you will come into contact with visiting teachers or advisers. Most schools have a liaison person concerned with the teaching of special needs. Various specialists will then visit, depending on the needs of the pupils, for example, an occupational therapist, a physiotherapist or a speech therapist. If you are working with a pupil with a particular need, then you should be included when that specialist comes to the school. The teacher may even delegate dealing with that visitor to you. These specialists will understand thoroughly the condition concerning the pupil, but will not know so much about the way the pupil has to work in school; so your partnership with them can be very supportive for the pupil. If, for instance, your charge has a hearing impairment, it makes sense that you know how to operate the hearing aids, what to do if things go wrong, and when your pupil needs the aids the most, or can get along without them. It makes sense that you learn sign language if that is used. It makes sense that you spend time on the practical things and liaise with the teacher later. You may have useful suggestions to make to either the teacher or the therapist. It will be a professional partnership. Do make notes of any meetings of this kind, date them and keep them in a secure place for reference. An ordinary exercise book with dated jottings would be fine, something you can share with the SENCO or a class teacher.

Documentation

While a handbook of some kind should be available for every member of staff, there will be differences depending on the category of staff for whom the handbook is intended. This should be a separate file to a personal portfolio, and will be the property of the school. It will be subject to updating. For some schools this will only be available electronically.

You should get your own copies of the following:

Its aims, philosophy and ethos.

The staff structure with roles and responsibilities of the class teacher, roles of senior staff, duties of ancillary staff including the role of the governing body, and the support staff Governor's name.

Basic school routines and procedures, e.g. registers, duties, marking, record keeping, reports, parents' evenings, sanctions, legal obligations (loco parentis) and health, safety and security.

The school policy for child protection, including the identity of the named person; the policy for confidentiality, and behaviour management.

Copies of relevant documentation for literacy and numeracy, and any other curriculum areas.

The school's SEN policy and arrangements for working with Individual Education Plans (IEPs), reviews and statemented children where appropriate.

Arrangements for staff meetings, working parties and consultations as relate to the TA.

Arrangements for line management, the whereabouts of pay, discipline and grievance documentation, union membership if desired.

Resources available in the school and how the TA should access them: stock and curricular equipment including SEN resources; the school library and ICT facilities including audio visual aids, e.g. television, radio, tapes, films, video etc.; reprographic equipment.

Resources available locally: curriculum development/teachers' centres, libraries, museums, field study centres etc.

(Watkinson 2008a: 171–172)

You should make sure you have the following information:

General staff guidance: confidentiality, expectations of dress, punctuality, code of courtesy etc.

Job descriptions, pay policy, discipline and grievance procedures

Role of governing body

Line management systems; staff structure; staff support systems

Professional development procedures

Fire and first aid practices; health and safety procedures, security, and off-site responsibilities

Behaviour policy: expectations, roles of all staff, responsibilities and strategies

Safeguarding children including child protection issues and procedures

Communication systems, including emergencies, bad weather, etc., rotas and timings, dates including meetings and agenda/minutes, newsletters from school

Systems for recording incidents or assessments where appropriate

Siting of relevant school policies and support materials

Equipment and resources: roles and responsibilities, access

Wet playtime procedures

(Watkinson 2008a: 172)

Curriculum and teaching policies

It is for the school to interpret how the NC and other activities are carried out in the school. The governors are responsible for seeing that this is done, and that the teachers do it properly. You help in this process. Sometimes it is difficult for a newcomer to pick up how to go about things. But much more is made explicit now, and less is left to chance or intuition. Databases and paperwork are used to record decisions and methods, and this is looked at in a school inspection. Not everything that happens in a school is set out in a written policy but more and more is, so that everyone can work in the same way. Schools will have a **curriculum policy**, laying out how and what is taught; and it is recommended that they have a **teaching and learning policy** to describe how teaching is to be done and what learning objectives are to be reached. Your role should be spelt out in these since you help 'deliver' the curriculum and assist the teaching and learning.

Other policies

You might like to look at some of the other policies with your teacher/mentor and some are essential for you to not only read, but understand and follow. Select a few that you think will be relevant to you and start there. First, find out where all the policies are kept. Then, when an interest or issue arises, you can go and look it up. This may be on an intranet rather than be paper based. The policies mentioned in the sections below – **Health and safety, Confidentiality, Child protection** and **Behaviour management** – are very relevant to your job: you should have your own copy of each of these. Try to take a look at the policy for **English and Mathematics,** as these come up in most other subjects, as does **ICT.** If you are supporting pupils with SEN, then the **SEN** policy is important. At some point you should take a look at policies to do with **pay and conditions of service,** and any covering **equal opportunities** or **inclusion, cultural diversity** and **anti-discrimination.** For those of you supporting pupils whose **home language is not English,** there will be a policy to help you with that.

Health and safety

As an employee you have a responsibility to be aware of potential dangers and to know what to do if there is a problem. This covers obvious things like fire alarms, the security of the building and grounds, and what to do about a blocked toilet; it also includes access to classrooms or playgrounds, and the storage of packed lunches to avoid food risks. All schools have these health and safety policies and there will be staff with special responsibilities to ensure the health and safety of all people in the premises: pupils, staff and visitors. The main emphases are on reasonableness and risk assessment. Some school buildings are old and difficult to make secure or accessible for wheelchairs. Others have worries with alarms and one-way entry doors, and you must familiarise yourself with these.

There will be a trained first aider in the school but they may not always be present when you need them. So firstly find out who they are and what you do if a pupil has an accident or is taken ill, then where the first aid materials are kept and what kind of things you are allowed to do. The use of first aid materials and the giving of prescription medicines will be restricted and subject to a school policy. This is to avoid giving or doing things to children or young people that could make matters worse – for instance, even allergies to plasters could elicit a severe reaction. It would be good if all school staff could attend a 1 day/6 hour course in emergency first aid (it would be good if all adults did!). The school may well buy in a trainer from the Red Cross or St John's Ambulance every so often so ask about this. Simple things can make the difference between life and death.

Do you know what to do if:

- the fire bell goes when you are in an unfamiliar part of the building?

- a pupil who is with you has a nose bleed/wets their pants/falls over/has an epileptic fit?

- it snows overnight?

- two pupils with you start swearing/fighting/run off?

- a pupil offers you a cigarette/dope/a hug?

- you are taken ill while alone with pupils?

- you find a damaged piece of equipment/graffiti?

- a pupil with you reveals something about their home circumstances/asks you to tea/asks how babies are made?

- you are asked to do a risk assessment?

Do discuss all of these with your mentor/line manager to make sure you are right.

Confidentiality in general

All members of staff, professionals and volunteers should maintain confidentiality about all that they see, hear or read while in school. You may wish a child received more attention at home, or was kept away from another child, but that cannot be said outside the professional dialogue with staff in the school. Likewise you should not comment about a child's progress – this is the teacher's job. Parents do approach TAs about their children, perhaps because they know you, or because you are less busy than the teachers. It is tempting to relay gossip to a friend, when you are dying to tell someone, so take great care.

Child protection

This is a sensitive and important area. All schools have written policies in this area and should ensure that all staff are trained together, but it is not always the case. If it does not happen in your school, then suggest it.

Teachers and other school staff act *in loco parentis*. The Children Acts apply to schools as well as the general population. The school policy should lay out clear guidelines for *all* staff on what to do if there is a suspicion of abuse, and on how to prevent allegations against staff themselves. I am sure you read about the deaths of Victoria Climbié and, more recently, Baby P that brought about the major changes under the Every Child Matters umbrella. There will be constant revision of the law and procedures within each local authority and institution in order to try to prevent such occurrences again.

There should be a designated senior person (DSP) whose name is known by all staff, who is trained in what to do and where to go if help is needed. It is important that you identify this person early on. Obtain a copy of the safeguarding policy, read it well and discuss it if you do not understand it on any point. The TDA induction material is very clear and useful on this subject and worth looking up on the internet if you are not able to attend the training sessions (TDA 2006a:, 2006b): 2.15 to 2.21.)

There are two main areas of sensitivity: recognising the signs of abuse; and behaving appropriately as a member of staff.

1 Signs of abuse

You should be aware of the possible signs of abuse. These are not always physical. Abuse can also be mental, or emotional, or be the result of neglect. This is not the place to describe all the signs and symptoms of abuse. You need some training from the LA Child Protection Officer (or whoever is responsible for it in your area). All children can have bruises from accidents or playing roughly. It is the type of bruise and where it is on the body that can be important. Do not be obsessive or inquisitive, but be vigilant – for instance when children change for PE (physical education), or are talking informally.

A child may reveal to you what has happened to them. You are particularly well placed for children to feel secure with you. You work in small groups or with individual pupils for periods of time and build up friendly relations. No school staff are trained to deal with children or families in detail, in child protection matters, but you all have a responsibility to recognise and report to people who are. Do not question a child in these circumstances, as you may ask leading questions; and never promise not to tell anyone. Listen carefully, sensitively, caringly, inwardly note what they say, and then tell the designated member of staff as soon as possible. Make a short written record afterwards, date it, and give it to this named member of staff. It is that person's responsibility to deal with it by informing Social Services or the police.

Incidents are rarely clear-cut. If you have any doubts about what you have heard or seen, discuss it with the class teacher, your teacher/mentor, the designated teacher or the head. If you are involved further, be guided by the named person in the school. These people will understand about case conferences, child protection registers, and agencies who can support vulnerable children and their families. Be sure to maintain confidentiality with the staff concerned, in all these proceedings.

2 Appropriate staff behaviour

The other area where you can be involved in child protection issues is when you are dealing with children in intimate situations. This may happen when dealing with pupils with physical disabilities, or very young children who have toileting accidents. Usually the parents know what the school policy is, whether school staff can clean children up after toilet accidents or change underclothes. TAs are often asked to work in pairs when these events occur. Always comfort unhappy children, but do it in public, not privately. There is no legislation against touching children but you should respond to them not initiate touching. Never put yourself into a situation that could lead to unjustified accusation. Children and young people can be very manipulative. Pupils need sometimes to see school as a haven, a place of safety and security that they may not otherwise have. Always be aware of, and respond to, troubled children, but recognise how to do this appropriately. Do not single them out for attention; it is better for them to come to you.

Another aspect of this policy can arise when dealing with difficult pupils. Restraining pupils can get you into difficulties with parents, and even the law. The pupils concerned are usually particularly volatile, liable to act up, or react unnecessarily to being told how to behave. Do make sure you know the school policy on restraint and, if possible, get appropriate training in this area. You should not be put in a difficult position with a pupil swearing in your face, being aggressive or dangerous to others in your early days in the school. If problems arise, make sure you talk immediately to your line manager. Most LAs have specialists in this area who can help.

Equal opportunities and related policies

Another policy area that affects the climate of the school is whether it provides equal opportunities for all. Schools have a duty to promote equality of opportunity and promote good relations between people of different groups. This does not necessarily mean equal provision. It means creating provision so that all have an equal opportunity to reach their potential. There will be a series of policies, all supporting equality provision, that cover how the school supports those with disabilities, those from different races or cultures, those with different gender and how the policies are monitored and how any incidents are reported.

In practice, it means considering how gender affects the way we behave towards one another. Gender barriers can be created unintentionally, say by always asking boys to move furniture or girls to clear up, or having pupils line up in boys' and girls' lines. You can also create opportunities for those of a different race or culture to contribute to the richness of school life. Show interest in them. Ask what hobbies they have got, what they do at the weekend, where they went for holidays. This will help you build up a relationship, and will also help others in the group to appreciate the variety of lifestyles. Encourage talk about clothes, ask to see photographs or pieces of fabric: these can range from football shirts to saris. Equal opportunities involves recognising achievement in academic and non-academic fields. You can play your part by promoting high standards for all, and recognising those strategies that promote self-esteem, prevent bullying and help pupils value one another.

Equality should be embedded in all of the school's policies and practices and permeate not only the treatment of pupils but the treatment of all associated with the school. Physically disabled people can be appointed as teachers, all support staff should be equally welcome in the staffroom and have their performance reviewed, social events can include governors and well as staff and so on. There is also a requirement now, which is inspected, for schools to actively promote community cohesion.

Discipline and behaviour management

There will be a clear school policy for this area and there are books dealing solely with this issue. Two easily readable ones by Bill Rogers might be a good start: *Classroom Behaviour* (Rogers 2006) and *Behaviour Management* (Rogers 2007) and so this book will not deal with it at length. This is also well dealt with in the TDA induction training. One of the keys to managing pupils' behaviour is to have all staff using a consistent way of dealing with whatever happens. There is no point you telling a pupil off for what you consider is inappropriate or unacceptable language or behaviour, if a teacher considers it acceptable. Likewise, if you are slacker than the teachers are, the pupils will behave badly with you and try to get away with things. Find out what rewards and sanctions you can use, and who to appeal to or send a pupil to if there is an incident you cannot deal with.

It is possible that in a few instances there will be a need for restraint procedures. Note the school policy about who can use these. It will be limited to a few people and you may become one, so do take note. These people will have special training to enable them to restrain a pupil otherwise out of control without hurting them or yourselves.

Some TAs are trained in counselling or using what is called circle time. These are strategies that attempt to defuse situations or even deal with them before they arise. Do not try to undertake these unless you are quite clear what you are doing and know what back-up there is if things go wrong. Counselling strategies try to get the pupils themselves to understand what has happened in a situation and how they might be able to deal with it differently in future. Circle time, where children only talk in the group if they are holding some kind of artefact, is a way of getting pupils to talk and listen to each other without interrupting. It is not a glorified 'newstime' as it has become in some schools, but properly used can enable pupils to open up in a secure environment and share problems they otherwise bottle up inside themselves. It is not a place for discussion or comment and can elicit quite sensitive issues – hence the health warning!

As part of a team, you should share concerns. This means you should:

- be caring and responsible;

- treat pupils and adults with respect;

- always try to ensure that there is a distinction between a pupil's behaviour and the pupil themselves when you deal with them (i.e. it is the behaviour that is bad, not the pupil);

- be honest and tolerant;

- control your temper and emotions; keep calm;

- ask for help or advice;

- be a professional.

A key area to consider is relationships. Test this by asking yourself the questions in the box. If any of your answers are unsatisfactory, is there anything you can do about it?

Questions about relationships in school

Is the school a happy place?

Are all staff consulted and involved in decision making in school?

How are pupils asked their opinions?

Can their views be used?

Are the children confident and relaxed when talking to staff?

Are differences of opinions, conflicts, etc. discussed openly in classrooms? the staffroom?

Do all staff feel valued members of the school?

How welcome do parents feel in the school?

How welcome do governors feel in the school?

Does the school reach out to those sections of the community/parents that are less involved in school?

What opportunities are there for parents and the school to share their hopes and expectations? How accessible is the head teacher to the pupils, the staff and the parents?

How accessible are staff to children, parents and governors?

How do we show that the opinions and help and support of parents and/or governors are valued? What opportunities are there for the pupils to link with the community?

Is there mutual respect?

What are you going to do if you have concerns in any of these areas?

Try to draw your school

No, not a scenic view, but an analogy.
Is it like a garden centre?

> Having a manager and staff, customers and a product. In schools the products are living things, all different with differing needs.

> There are fertilisers and pest controllers (curricula and resources) and . . .

Or is it a stage?

> With performers and an audience
> producer and backstage staff
> script writer and critics.

> Practice makes perfect . . . Can you repeat the same thing day in and day out – or . . .

Or a ship?

> With a captain and crew, passengers of various kinds
> in rough seas and calm ones
> needing fuel and equipment
> could be of varying ages.

> Does it navigate by the stars or with a compass . . .?

Or . . .?

What is learning?

THE PURPOSE OF a school is to enhance learning, hopefully not only in the pupils but also in all those who make up the school's team. Teaching is the process by which the learning is enhanced. I have deliberately put these two chapters about learning and teaching before the more practical ones. These days, TAs are so much more than dog's bodies and paint-pot washers. To be proactive rather than reactive, some basic theories and principles underpinning the practice are really important in helping you make the most of your assisting role. To teach, you need to know how pupils learn.

Learning is complex and only partly understood even by those who spend their life trying to make sense of it. The shelves of the library are heavy with research and books explaining what is meant by learning, and how it can best happen, how to improve it or speed it up. Teaching is not just a question of 'delivering' the curriculum. The brain is not an empty jug into which knowledge can be poured. A useful way to start trying to understand the process of learning is to look at how you yourself learn. Use the exercise to help you do this. If your colleagues are willing, ask them about their experiences.

How do you learn?

Recall a recent learning experience. It can be a formal one such as a course or evening class; a life experience such as coping with family changes, bringing up children, even divorce or bereavement; using a new piece of equipment such as a new video recorder or learning to drive. The context does not matter, but you need to remember it fairly clearly.

The exercise has been used by adults on courses and some of their jottings are shown below. Were your experiences similar to these?

1 **Reasons given for undertaking the learning:**
   new teacher – accident – thought it would be fun – thought I needed it – to keep up – needed to.

2 **Things people said had helped:**
   friends – time – previous knowledge – resources – sharing experience – fun – patience – mistakes.

3 **Emotions people experienced:**
   anxiety – frustration – challenge – fear – sense of achievement – empathy – patience – loneliness.

4 **Needs experienced during the learning process:**
   initial interest – motivation – self-determination – time and breaks, or space – commitment – structure – someone to help – a teacher (a bossy tutor was appreciated later) – a mentor – practical experience (doing) – self-discipline – social intercourse (group working, others alongside).

Looking at yourself as a learner

Just jot down a few things about that experience, describing it briefly:

What made you undertake it?

Why did you do it?

Was it necessity or whim?

Or?

What or who helped you start?

What or who helped you during the process?

What or who hindered during the process?

Was it the same all the way through?

If not, how did it vary?

What else would have helped or could have been done to help you?

What feelings did you have during the process?

What skills and knowledge did you acquire?

Did anything you did or learnt relate to anything else in your life?

Have you finished? If not, will it finish?

What would you change now with hindsight?

It is possible to draw up a set of principles with help from this exercise and lists like these. You will notice:

- Learning is not a straightforward process. It has ups and downs, and even goes backwards at times.

- People can help and hinder.

- Another person who has more experience of the same area usually is helpful – this may be a teacher or a course tutor but does not have to be.

- Other life experiences always help somewhere.

- Correct tools or words or strategies usually help.

- Time and timing is important, as are challenge and motivation.

- Most learners experience fear and anxiety as well as satisfaction.

- Attitudes to learning are important.

- Learning rarely finishes, even in a restricted area, even if the course itself does.

- We go on learning all our lives.

Trying to define learning is hard in itself. The dictionary puts the emphasis on getting more knowledge, but learning is not just about acquiring facts. One quite useful definition is: 'Learning . . . that reflective activity which enables the learner to draw upon previous experience, to understand and evaluate the present, so as to shape future action and formulate new knowledge' (Abbott 1996: 1. One problem is that learning itself cannot be seen, only the behaviour that happens after it has taken place. There are the heart-stopping moments of seeing the 'penny drop', but these do not constitute all that is going on; most of it you cannot see. Figure 4.1 illustrates the process of learning and some of the factors that surround it. The rest of the chapter gives you further details about each of the boxes in the diagram.

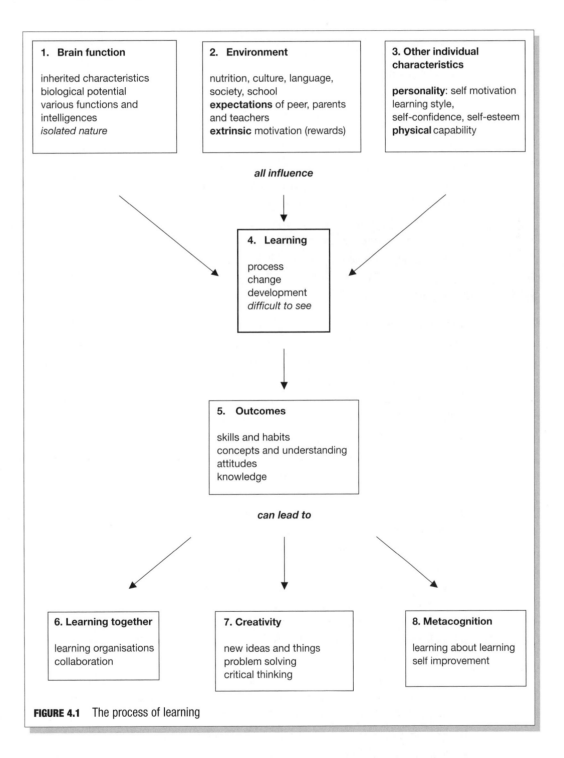

FIGURE 4.1 The process of learning

1 The brain

Learning is a process of change taking place in the brain. (Human beings are animals with highly developed brains.)

The inherited learning tools

The brain is made up of

> billions of cells, (neurones). The total length of its 'wiring' between the neurones is about 100,000 kilometres (62,150 miles) . . . the memory capability could be compared to 1000 CD ROMs each one containing an Encarta encyclopaedia . . . the layers of organisation within the brain that act together apparently miraculously, . . . handle not only memory but also vision, learning, emotion and consciousness.
>
> (Abbott 1997: 3)

These billions of cells meet up with each other and form enormous networks. The brain pathways between them are more complicated than any known computer and these pathways are in constant action, carrying messages (impulses) to the cells. Given the number of cells, and the number of possible pathways, the potential for learning is vast. Given the intricate layout, it is no wonder that learning and enabling learning are complex processes. If you have had a relative or friend who suffered a stroke, you will know that it may be possible to redirect the messages along different pathways, so that the patient relearns how to walk or talk. But it takes time to do so.

Systems for learning

The brain functions at all sorts of levels to control the things we do. There are the automatic systems that control breathing and heart rate – we don't have to think about these. There are the more controllable yet reflex movements such as those that enable us to escape harm – pulling your hand away from a flame for instance. And then there are what some people call the higher order levels of brain activity, such as the emotions, our memory and thinking.

Practising can move some activities to a more automatic or reflex level. Learning to play a musical instrument or drive a car involves practicing certain routines so that they become automatic, so that the brain can concentrate on the higher order aspects that require thought. Some school learning needs this kind of approach: pupils repeat things in order to make them second nature. PE routines, tables and spellings fall into this category. Some pupils need more repetition than others to make these routines what we refer to as 'second nature' – automatic. A TA can do useful work here repeating some things with those who learn slowly, while the teacher goes on to the next thing for those who learn more quickly. You can try to find different ways of tackling the repetition to stop it becoming boring. Lots of praise is needed, that is the reward. It also helps to break the tasks down into even smaller steps for some pupils; the reward is getting them to recognise that achieving each small step is a milestone for them. Schools sometimes use tangible rewards such as stickers but usually real praise is enough for school work. But beware – pupils soon know if you are saying 'well done' when it isn't deserved.

When teachers draw up IEPs for children with special learning needs, this is exactly what they are doing – breaking the learning down into small steps that the learner can achieve. They set these as targets, sharing them with the pupil so that the pupil can recognise when progress has been made, and celebrate it. By working with the teacher over these IEPs, either helping to write them, sharing them with the pupils, doing the work with them or celebrating the achievement, you are helping the pupils make progress in their learning. For more detail about IEPs and the learning of youngsters with special learning needs you are recommended to read one of the specialist books in this series.

Growth and learning

The brain grows and develops like any other part of the body. There are stages in *physical* development that, as a parent, you will easily recognise or remember from your own growing up. Our *emotions* also develop, as do our ability to make relationships (*social* development), our understanding of our *culture,* and our ability to appreciate *spiritual* things.

Looking at physical child development

Get out photos or videos of your family.

Can you tell by looking at these how old the children are?

Try them out on friends who do not know your children.

What do you look for?

In the early stages, you can see whether they can sit up or walk You may notice how big the head is in comparison with the rest of the body Later, you will know whether they are wearing nappies still or how many teeth have come through.

Thinking and learning develop as we grow, and go through stages. As with other aspects of development, the stages are not fixed. Some children never crawl; feet size can develop before height catches up. Some children talk all at once in sentences while others seem to gain a wide vocabulary first. Development can go in fits and bursts, and can sometimes seem to stay still. Piaget, an educationalist who influenced school methods for many years, studied the stages of intellectual (cognitive) development, giving them technical names that you may still hear mentioned in schools today, particularly primary or nursery schools.

Piaget's developmental stages of concept development are still useful when considering how to help children learn:

- Up to about 18 months old infants are involved in developing skills of mobility and sensing their environment; this is the 'sensori-motor stage'.

- From 2 to 4 years children are concerned only with themselves (egocentric); this is the 'pre-operational stage'.

- By about 4, children are at the 'intuitive' stage – thinking logically but unaware of what they are doing.

- From 7 to 11 years old, children can operate logically, but still need to see and work with real objects to learn and understand; this is the 'concrete stage'.

- Then the child is capable of 'formal' thinking about things without the 'props'; this is the 'abstract' stage.

Early learning, Piaget said, depends on using our senses: tasting, smelling, touching, seeing and hearing, and moving about to explore the world. Have you noticed how toddlers put everything in their mouths?

Early learning for 2- to 4-year-olds is largely practical and experience based. Children start to play together, so playgroups and nurseries help them move away from thinking only about themselves. Nursery activities are practical, acknowledging that small children need to experience the world to make sense of it, to put meaning to the words they use, before they can make sense of reading and writing and counting.

The 5- to 7-year-olds (Key Stage 1) need practical activities, and lots of learning through play. These classrooms are full of apparatus and equipment. It may well be part of your job to maintain this. As you become familiar with the materials, notice when the children use the equipment. It is not just for entertaining them or keeping them quiet. Sand and water trays, role play areas, jigsaws and so on help children grasp fundamental concepts on which to build the rest of their learning.

Going from Key Stage 1 to Key Stage 2, to the 7- to 11-year olds, children still need 'props' for their learning: blocks for counting, artefacts, films about days gone by. When you work with children in Key Stage 2 who have learning problems, remember their learning will depend much more on props than that of others in the class. Slower learners may need counters or coins to help with their calculations and pictures in their reading books to help them enjoy the stories. They still need to play with art media and have time to develop. But it is not just slow learners who need these experiences. We need to give all children ideas and facts in stages, and provide them with props and practical experiences where possible. Even as adults we go through similar stages. We play or fiddle about with new tools or media and try things out until we have absorbed, or assimilated, the idea.

Much science work in schools is based on Piaget's ideas. There have been several research projects such as *Children Learning in Science* (Driver 1983), *Really Raising Standards* (Adey and Shayer 1994) and SPACE (Science Processes and Concept Exploration) research (Russell and McGuigan 1991) to look at the way young people learn science. The NC for science was firmly based on the ideas of stages in conceptual development described by such work. The Adey and Shayer work continues to this day. The science teachers in your school may be able to discuss these ideas with you. The old series Science 5–13 (Learning through Science 1980) and the Nuffield Primary Science series (Nuffield, Primary, and Science 1967) are unlikely to

Gardner's intelligences

Verbal/linguistic:

Do you think in words? Do you have to talk or write things down to sort them out? Logical/mathematical: Do you like things organised? Are you good at numbers?

Visual/spatial: Do you think in pictures? Do you like diagrams? Can you visualise things easily when you read about them?

Bodily/kinaesthetic: Are you good at PE? Have people described you as agile or the opposite – clumsy?

Musical/rhythmic: Are you musical? Do you like dancing? Do you work better with music playing in the background?

Interpersonal: Do you get on well with other people? Do you form relationships easily? Do you work better with others?

Intrapersonal: Can you work things out for yourself or do you have to always involve others? Are you comfortable with yourself? Can you work on your own?

be on staffroom shelves these days as so much will be used directly based on the Qualifications and Curriculum Authority (QCA) schemes of work but both were schemes based on the research about stages of development. SPACE materials are still on education library shelves and well used.

Learning styles

There are differences in the physical make-up of individual brains, even in identical twins. It is also believed that different parts of the brain engage in different ways of thinking or learning. Some of this can now even be seen in living brains with the use of magnetic resonance imaging (MRI) scanning techniques. Gardner and colleagues (1996) suggest in their book *Intelligence: Multiple perspectives* that there is not just one intelligence, but seven. He says there are different intelligences for different things but you can be good in more than one area. Try out the list of Gardner's intelligences on yourself.

If you can find out how you work best you can use that method when you have to learn something new. You can also try to develop aspects of yourself that you feel are weak. So if you are not good at working with others you might try to develop this skill. If you are musical, you may find it easier to learn with music playing, or you might even turn a list of things you have to learn into a song!

Likewise, it might be helpful for the pupils you work with to sort out their strengths and weaknesses. Talk to them about it. The idea is that if we know what mode the pupils are operating in we can support them better.

2 The world around us

The influence of environment

Outside influences can also affect how our learning develops. For example, differences in language affect how we communicate, and the words we use. Even English language vocabulary differs between the United Kingdom and the United States. Children from homes where there are few books and little discussion are likely to have a restricted vocabulary. They may not be able to label and describe as many things and ideas as children from families where self-expression is encouraged. Similarly they may be less fluent with grammar and structure. One of the important roles a TA can play is to extend children's vocabulary and enable them to express their views and ideas better.

Changes of background, language or culture can create barriers to learning. Names you may hear in the staffroom will include Bernstein, Bruner and Vygotsky (Wood 1998). Changes in routines can affect day-to-day learning. Emotional and social context will affect learning processes. Even things such as the goldfish dying or Auntie coming to stay can upset the learning process for some pupils. This means you need to be sensitive to the background of the pupils you work with. You cannot change their circumstances, but if you are aware of them you will have a greater understanding of the pupil's learning needs. It may be that you are the one member of staff they can confide in when they cannot concentrate, or seem tired or off colour. Do remember to tell the teacher you are working with if you are at all bothered by what a pupil tells you, or if you think the problem is likely to be a long-standing one. There was more about dealing with worrying confidences in chapter 3.

Social interaction or lack of it can affect learning. As we have seen, this may be a language problem; but it is also about relating to other people, learning with and from them, and communicating. Playgroups and nurseries help children develop socially before they come into mainstream school, where for so much of their time they are confined to a desk or table.

As a TA, working with small groups you are an important factor in helping pupils develop both social skills to enable them to get on with one another and social awareness to help them learn.

3 The world inside us – our physical status, personality, motivation and learning

Similarities and differences

If we are tired or ill it can be hard to learn, even just to read. Children and young people with a physical disability are liable to have to spend effort and time in dealing with the disability – effort and time that the able-bodied can put into learning. All who work with pupils with special educational needs of a physical origin will be familiar with the effects these disabilities can have. Your role will be to provide the support that takes away some of the hassle their physical condition brings, so that they can use their mental powers to the full. In the photograph a TA is transporting an able pupil over lengthy distances between teaching areas. Once in the teaching area he can concentrate on what he has to do and cope with the walking necessary in the classroom.

There are also children whose brains are damaged or underdeveloped. This may prevent them from thinking and learning properly. Try to discuss these two types of physical disability with the class teacher whose class has SEN children in it, or the SENCO. Children with a

PHOTOGRAPH 4.1   Helping a student to keep all his energies for the classroom

physical impairment can think and learn as well as other children if they are given the appropriate support. But a different kind of help is needed for children with brain damage. Fortunately, much can now be done to assist their learning.

Abilities, competencies, intelligences all run on spectrums. Just as there are children who have disabilities there will be some whose brains work faster than others and some who have special talents. As all children are different genetically – except identical twins (and even they have differing experiences even in the womb) – matching the curriculum to individual needs seems impossible. Luckily, most children develop at roughly the same rate, and organising schools in year groups makes sense. But clearly, if the teaching is geared to the broad average, those who are at either end of the spectrum are going to miss out. It is here that TAs can be of great help. However, it can easily happen that you, the least experienced and possibly the least well prepared and trained, may be asked to deal with the most challenging and needy pupils. Recent years have seen an increase in the number of children with special needs and disabilities in mainstream schools. Many have been very successfully included because of people like you, but you do need to make sure you know what the needs are and that your help is not actually excluding the pupil from being part of the class or group, or labelling them as different.

Make sure you talk with the SENCO or inclusion manager about your role, as well as each class teacher that you work with. It is not good enough that you are seen by a class teacher as automatically solving a difficult problem for the teacher without support. This also goes for helping those who are gifted and talented. Too often it is expected that because they are bright they can get on without adult help. They need encouragement and challenge just as much as any other child, sometimes more so.

Emotional development

Emotional development and conditions affect learning. Much greater recognition of this in recent years is largely due to the work of Goleman (1996). The SEAL (Social and Emotional Attitudes to Learning) materials are really helpful in developing a greater understanding of children's needs and their understanding of themselves. Just type 'SEAL materials' into a search engine or go to the DCSF Standards' or National Strategies' sites to find the full details. The materials also give longer explanations of the importance of attitudes to learning.

Feelings can get in the way, and pupils – even bright ones – who are bored, insecure or preoccupied by other problems, will not perform well. Younger children are less able to control these emotions, and teenagers' control systems are affected by hormones. You can be of great help to the learning situation by providing an understanding ear to pupils in distress and sharing the information with the class teacher.

Motivation

Motivation is one of the greatest influences on learning. The will to achieve can overcome many physical and social handicaps. Look at the effort that goes into the paraplegic Olympics. Setting up a home of one's own can make 'DIY' experts of even the most impractical people. The opposite also applies: when one becomes bored it is difficult to concentrate or persevere. Even easy tasks become a chore.

One of the skills you can develop is to find out the interests of your pupils, and build upon them. Find a football annual, a handbook on guinea pig care or get an internet guide, if that is what they want to read about. They are much more likely to read something of use or interest to them. Having a purpose for writing – a story for younger children to read, or a thank you letter can be more motivating than an invented task. Drama can be a way through to literature, performance a way to music. The outdoor environment, working with living things or physical activity can be very motivating. Practical work is usually much more interesting and involving for pupils than a worksheet. Always keep a note of any changes you make and share them with the teacher.

Self-confidence and self-esteem

This was sometimes overlooked in the past. We all have stories from our own schooldays of the teacher who was demeaning of our efforts. A put-down can occasionally motivate a pupil to achieve despite the comment, but the memory of discomfort stays. Many others are prevented by failure, or even perceived failure, from trying a second time. We all need to be valued. Lack of self-esteem does not always relate to poor performance but to an individual's self-image. Highly successful people can have a poor self-concept; it does not always show as depression or withdrawal. Your feedback is crucial to the pupil. Show how to do things by example, but don't overwhelm pupils with your own talent! Try some of the following:

Do you use any of these strategies that could raise self-esteem? Watch other staff and see what happens when they use them.

Talk to everyone the same way, regardless of gender, race or background.

Address pupils by their preferred name.

Use positive comments – 'thank you for walking' – 'well done for being quiet', including written comments if you can – 'well read today' – 'I liked the story'.

Use praise appropriately, not indiscriminately. Over-praising defeats the object.

Treat boys and girls equally, whether for tasks or treats or even lining up.

Provide a good role model in gender, culture and disability, both in reality and when finding examples in teaching materials such as books and magazines.

Use rewards, praise and congratulation systems for work, including showing it to other staff.

Catch them being good or working hard and tell them.

Set small achievable targets and congratulate them on achieving them.

Have reward systems for behaviour – telling the teachers about the good as well as the troublesome.

Value work by ensuring it is taken care of, and presented well, both by you and the pupil.

Encourage independence appropriate to age and maturity.

Enable and encourage peer tutoring.

Use humour carefully.

Encourage children to value their own performance.

Listen to the views of pupils and act on them where possible.

Avoid being patronising or sarcastic as pupils recognise both.

Can you add to this list?

4 The actual process of learning – what is taking place

Observing learning

The learning process is a subject of much research by people trying to explain how it happens so that we can accelerate it. One of the exciting things when working with children is to see that 'penny drop' moment, but it is only a small part of the story. Learning is built up from lots of little pieces. Educational psychologists spend much time trying to work out the learning patterns of children who are struggling with school work. This can be a fascinating area, but you have to recognise that there are no easy answers or short cuts. Just keep watching, listening and learning more about learning.

Try spending a little time watching other learners. To do this you will need the cooperation of a class teacher with whom you can discuss the issues and protocols of observation. You will notice all sorts of things at random, just by being in a busy classroom, but it will sharpen your perceptions if you do this with some organisation. It means either taking time out of your paid time or using your own time. It is important that your observing does not become intrusive for the pupil. You will need to make some notes, and this means making records on someone else's child, and for whom a class teacher is responsible. These matters must not be taken lightly, so you need some agreed ground rules.

Check the following:

- the purpose of your observation;

- confidentiality of things said;

- ownership of things written;

- what is left unsaid – honesty and integrity will help;

- ethical factors involved by mentioning others in your school or family;

- whether names are to be used or records to be anonymised;

- what happens to any discussions or records.

Possible protocols to consider for classroom observation

The following needs to be discussed between you and the class teacher where any observation is to take place:

- The purpose of the exercise is to . . . (e.g. understand more about).

- The adults involved will be . . .

- The pupils involved will be . . .

- The head teacher/department head/line manager has been told what is happening, and has agreed.

It needs to be checked that:

- Anything written is shared first with the teacher for comments to be made and points of accuracy checked.

continued . . .

- Any comments to be seen by others will be anonymised, or amalgamated with others to preserve confidentiality.

- The main audience of any summary written material would be . . . (e.g. the other member of a course, or an outside reader).

- The people observed or interviewed can have a copy of the notes made if they so wished.

- You know what will happen to any written records.

- The intended outcome of the activity is . . .

- You know what you will do if the observation shows up anything within the classroom or school that someone wishes to address or celebrate.

- If others get involved, they would be covered by the same sort of protocols.

- Someone seeks permission of the parents of the children closely involved.

- Either side can make comments at any time in the process if there is any discomfort or suggestion about what is taking place or being said.

There are books that cover why, what, where and how to observe, such as Wragg (1999) – although this was written for teachers – and Harding and Meldon-Smith (1996). This latter book was written for NVQ (National Vocational Qualification) students in Child Care and so is a more helpful book for TAs. Even though written primarily for those working with very young children, its principles hold good throughout school phases, and the suggested forms are very useful. These books also look at things you can measure about learning and things that you cannot, but that are equally important.

It is really important that you practise observing as it is a skill that will help you throughout your career in education. Try honing your skills when out for a walk, just make a practice of noticing things. Practically in class, you will need a means of writing and something to record on. A sheet of A4 paper on a clipboard will do, or a spiral bound memo pad. Probably the most difficult decision is where to start, with so many things happening at once in any classroom. The trick is to focus on one area of interest and observe at regular times. The exercises in the boxes should get you started.

Observing a pupil (1)

Remembering the protocols of observing, with the agreement of the class teacher and, if possible, the pupil you watch:

- Decide on a pupil to watch.

- Decide on a part of their body that is of interest – their hands? What they are saying?

- Note what is happening every minute on the minute for five minutes.

- Did they keep still?

- Did they touch any resources?

- Did they touch another pupil?

- Who did they speak to? Was it about their work?

Did this tell you anything more about the pupil, the resources they are working with, the children they are with? Repeat the exercise with a different pupil at the same desk/table, or the same pupil in a different context or classroom.

Observing a pupil (2)

Remembering the protocols of observing, with the agreement of the teacher and, if possible, the pupil:

- Mark out a sheet of A4 with headings for five-minute intervals covering half an hour.

- Choose a pupil that you are not working directly with.

- Note every five minutes what they are doing.

- If they are talking and you can hear what they say, put that down.

- What have you found out about this pupil?

Observation is often the way to 'catch a pupil being good'. If you are observing a pupil who is frequently a problem, notice what they were occupied with when they were not distracting someone else. When they are distracting others, note down what started it off, and what makes it worse or better. You can develop grids with names and headings of what you are particularly looking for, such as asking or answering questions, or with time markers.

After you have done the observation, ask yourself the following questions.

After observing

- What did the pupil do during that period?

- Was it anything to do with what the teacher intended or not?

- Did the pupil learn anything new during the time you were watching?

- Did they understand anything better?

- Did they practise anything that they had done before?

- Did anyone talk to them or help them?

- If so, were these people sitting near them or adults?

- Could you have made things easier for them if you had been sitting there, or if they had been in a different place, or had different resources?

- In what ways?

- Find an opportunity to talk through what you saw with the teacher.

There is some material on observation in the TDA induction materials but much of it is geared to watching the teacher's behaviour in literacy or mathematics lessons rather than watching how the pupils learn. It is important before observing to be sure of your own objectives. The objectives stated in the induction materials in the Role and Context modules are what you would do every day both in primary and secondary schools. They are to:

- provide reliable information of pupils' progress on the curriculum;

- identify pupils' strengths and weaknesses;

- discover how well pupils are responding to the teaching resources;

- enable feedback to pupils on what they need to do to progress;

- enable feedback to teachers on the response of pupils to the work.

(TDA 2006a, 2006b: 2.34)

However, the primary TAs' induction training has a module entitled 'Understanding How Children Learn'. Secondary TAs need this just as much so if you are working or intending to work in this sector. So see if you can have a look at the primary materials or even attend the session. Much of the session involves watching video material of children at different primary ages and stages, a very useful introduction to the subject. Much of what you can observe are the behaviours associated with the learning process rather than what is actually happening in the pupil's head, but it all helps understand the context of successful learning. The presentation slide 3.2 gives a list of the key things one can learn about the actual process from such observations:

Slide 3.2

- Learning is an active process

- Each pupil is unique, having their own experiences, skills, understanding, knowledge and preferred approaches to learning

- Language plays a key role in learning

(TDA 2006a: 3.5)

By active, the statement does not mean physical movement on the part of the learner but that the learner has to be engaged with the process – you cannot 'do learning' to another. Teaching is about enabling learning to take place.

5 Learning a range of things: facts (knowledge), how to do things (skills), better understanding (concepts) and about ourselves (attitudes)

What is learnt?

It might seem easier to observe and measure what is learnt over a period of time rather than try to watch it actually happening, but it has its pitfalls. Test results depend very much on how questions are asked, particularly where understanding is needed as well as memory recall, as in a subject such as science. Pictures, and seeing or being able to handle the materials about which questions are asked – even being able to ask questions about the meaning of the questions – all alter how correct the answers may be.

Teachers plan for a particular outcome and therefore know what they are looking for. Work with the teacher to understand this and you too will be able to see when those you are helping have 'got there'. By practising and refining your observations of learning, in a particular area or with a particular child, you can record what you have seen, and give valuable feedback to the teacher. This means teachers *can* have eyes in the backs of their heads, can teach and keep a check on the pupils, can do two things at once.

The outcomes of learning are not all factual knowledge. Most important is the understanding that goes with the facts. There are the skills and habits that come from repeating tasks, from practising. A musician or gymnast, a carpenter or mechanic will tell you of the hours they have spent perfecting skills, however talented they are in the field. It is also important to look at pupils' attitudes to learning.

6 Learning together can result in greater achievements than learning in isolation

Learning together

Interestingly, when two or three people are working together, the result can be better than their individual efforts might produce. People working in groups or teams can bounce ideas off one another; come with different learning styles, different sets of competencies and skills, experiences and knowledge bases that contribute to the whole. Individual learning is essential, but joint learning can be not only productive but exciting, developmental and creative. This is true for the children and adults.

It is important to distinguish whether children in a group are all doing similar but individual tasks or whether they are doing a collaborative task where each member can contribute something to the whole. In the first of these, more work may be done if there is silence, but in the second, talking together is essential. Working with groups is dealt with in Chapter 6.

7 What is learnt can lead to thinking and creating new ideas or solving problems

The areas of thinking, creativity and problem solving are ones where there is a lot of debate. Some teachers feel the legally required NC, the strategy instructions or the schools' syllabuses leave little time for these activities. Other teachers ensure they earmark time or provide after school activities that give opportunities for these areas to be covered. While not all learning needs to result in creative or problem-solving activity, it is here that the greatest achievements of human beings are born. Without these activities, there would have been no civilisations, no progress, no arts or technical advances. It is important to establish with the class teacher to what extent you may allow the pupils you are working with to deviate from the task in hand if they get a good idea.

8 Learning about learning helps people improve their own learning strategies

If we can recognise how we best learn – our style – we can build on that knowledge. We can also train ourselves to improve. It is partly about understanding the different intelligences mentioned before, but it is also about all the other pieces in the learning jigsaw: when help is needed, whether there are emotional or physical things stopping the process, what kind of tools, books or equipment will help with a task, what kind of words might help. If you want to read more about learning try *Psychology for Teaching Assistants* (Arnold and Yeomans 2005). A fun book about learning with lots of soundbites and drawings is *The New Learning Revolution* by Dryden and Vos (2005).

Learning about learning is called **metacognition**. You can help your pupils to recognise how they best learn. You can recognise your own learning patterns and watch for patterns in the pupils with whom you work. Try talking to the children about what you have seen. Use phrases suh as 'Are you are reading through your written work?', 'Where do you do your homework?', 'Would singing your spellings help you learn them?'.

Using your understanding to assist learning

To help assist learning you can:

- try to understand more about your own learning styles;

- provide opportunities for repetition and reinforcement, vocabulary and scaffolding;

- learn more about the social, cultural or emotional context in which the pupils are operating;

- find out more about the individual needs of the pupils with whom you are working closely;

- find out what experiences the learners have already had or what they might have missed;

- learn something of the subjects that they are learning for yourself, so that you know what might be coming next, or know what an appropriate strategy for that subject might be;

- notice what kind of learning styles pupils have and talk with them about their own learning;

- value pupils and their learning, appreciate what individuals have achieved and tell them – to boost their self-esteem;

- be authentic, open, with pupils and adults;

- ensure you know what is the learning intention of the teacher;

- assist in creating a positive learning environment, both in the material surroundings and in attitudes to work and one another;

- become part of the learning organisation that is your school, share your ideas and listen to others;

- apply your learning to the situation in which you find yourself;

- have high expectations of the pupils, yourself and learning standards.

What is teaching?

ASK YOUR TA and teacher colleagues what they mean by 'teaching'. They may use the word 'pedagogy', the art or study of teaching. Watkins and Mortimore (1999) define pedagogy as 'any conscious activity by one person designed to enhance the learning in another' (p. 3). We all teach at some time. Parents teach their children, children teach other children. But by 'teachers', the government, the general public, and more particularly the media, are referring to adults with qualified teacher status. Most dictionary definitions of teaching can be applied to the work of TAs, but they could also be used about many other categories of people interacting with children. We need to look at educational definitions.

Teachers may refer you to the definition used by Ofsted inspectors. While these inspectors are not required to look directly at the work of TAs in the classroom using their framework, unless they are HLTAs in charge of a class, but some do so out of interest. They have remarked that TAs can score highly using similar criteria to those used for teachers. As you read the following you immediately see that the Ofsted definition of good teaching is shown by how the learners learn:

> Learners make good progress and show good attitudes to their work, as a result of effective teaching. The teachers' good subject knowledge lends confidence to their teaching styles, which engage all groups of learners and encourage them to work well independently. Classes are managed effectively. Learners respond to appropriate challenges. Based on thorough and accurate assessment that helps learners to improve, work is closely tailored to the full range of learners' needs, so that all can succeed including those with learning difficulties and/or disabilities. Learners are guided to assess their work themselves. Teaching assistants and other classroom helpers, and resources, are well deployed to support learning. Good relationships support parents and carers in helping learners to succeed.
>
> (Ofsted 2009: 15, 16)

Another source of a definition worth looking at can be found in the published standards for qualified teachers, which you will find on the TDA website. These make it clear there is much more to being a teacher than the front-of-class role; but they are detailed and, for some, controversial. They also give gradations of competency for the various senior levels of teacher.

The 2003 Regulations concerning teachers define qualified teacher status and what teachers should and should not do. They define, in Regulation 6, the 'specified work' of teaching as:

(a) planning and preparing lessons and courses for pupils;

(b) delivering lessons to pupils;

(c) assessing the development, progress and attainment of pupils; and

(d) reporting on the development, progress and attainment of pupils.

[delivery includes distance learning or computerised techniques.]

(DfES 2003a: 3)

It is the associated regulations that distinguish 'teachers' from 'TAs'. A person who is not a qualified teacher may carry out work specified in the above definition only if the following conditions are satisfied –

(a) he carries out work specified in section 6 in order to assist to support the work of a qualified teacher or a nominated teacher in the school;

(b) he is subject to the direction and supervision of such a qualified teacher or nominated teacher in accordance with arrangements made by the headteacher of the school; and

(c) the headteacher is satisfied that he has the skills, expertise and experience required to carry out work specified in regulation 6.

(DfES 2003a): 10

Books by Kyriacou (2007, 2009) called *Essential Teaching Skills* and *Effective Teaching in Schools* are very readable. Dunne and Wragg's (1994) *Effective Teaching* is also very accessible and short. All would be helpful to dip into and discuss with teachers about the nature of your job. You may find these in your staffroom, or teacher colleagues may have a copy to lend. It isn't necessary to read them in detail, but all contain some useful definitions and tasks to do, as well as amusing drawings and helpful photographs. If your teachers are familiar with them, ask them which bits they found helpful.

Remember that the classroom teacher must lead in setting out the objectives of the lessons and the strategies by which these can be achieved, provide the role model and direct the activities. Given this lead, you can assist in all of these areas, provided you and the teacher are agreed about your boundaries. TAs do teach, but do not carry the responsibility for the direction and organisation of the learning.

Yet another way of thinking about the teaching process is to consider it as an integration of models, skills and artistry (Hopkins 1995) (see Figure 5.1).

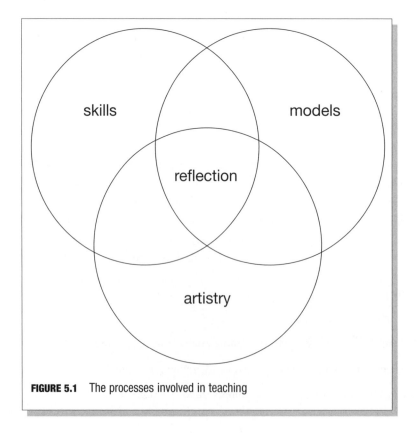

FIGURE 5.1 The processes involved in teaching

Models

The term 'models' refers to different teaching approaches, such as:

- didactic or instructional – the 'stand up in front of a group and tell them' approach;

- group working – pupils of the same ages (peers) cooperating to further their learning;

- creative – allowing pupils to create, experiment and investigate beyond the set work;

- mechanical – encouraging the memorising of things such as spellings or tables, or old-fashioned 'object' lessons

and so on. It is generally agreed that all teachers need to use a combination of styles or approaches to tackle the variety of subjects they teach and pupils' various needs. This is how they achieve the 'match' between the pupils and the curriculum. The literacy and numeracy strategies include all these various approaches through a lesson or session.

You are unlikely to need to use these different styles certainly to begin with, since you will not be dealing with whole classes or whole lessons.

Try to watch various teachers at work and see how they approach their teaching.

Is it different for different subjects? For instance, do drama or PE teachers favour one approach, or science or technology teachers another?

Do the teachers of younger children teach in the same way as the teachers of older children?

Do all teachers spend the same sort of time talking to the whole class?

How often do they use a whiteboard or an interactive board and how do they use it?

What kind of demonstrations do they give?

What opportunities are there for pupils to express their own ideas? Ask questions?

Artistry

Artistry is about using personality and relationships to create the right learning atmosphere for the situation. For some, it appears completely instinctive – maybe these are the 'born teachers'. On the other hand, artistry can be cultivated and developed by those teachers and TAs who are themselves learners – those who reflect upon their own practice and continually refine what they do.

Personality

Never underestimate the effect you as a TA have on a classroom climate just by being you. Watching TAs at work with children and young people, it is clear that the way they relate to the pupils has a powerful effect on the learning. You need to be *sensitive* to changes in pupils' moods, and to respond appropriately.

A TA is a role model for learning and can show that learning never stops. You also offer a role model for good manners, for care of equipment, for the way you organise the resources, for the way you talk to one another. Even your speech and handwriting offer exemplars, hopefully of the way the school wants their pupils to go. Your clothes give messages – the right shoes for PE, the aprons for practical work all show the proper way of doing things. You can role model learning itself by asking questions when you do not understand, and by talking about any reading or training that you are undertaking.

The following are characteristics of TAs that have been noted in the classroom. Do they describe you?

Enthusiasm   Your enthusiasm, interest and love of your job, your enjoyment of their company alone can improve the interest and enjoyment for pupils and their motivation.

Listening skills   Can you listen? For some children just having someone to talk to can make all the difference.

Self-confidence   Your confidence – acting it, even if you are scared underneath – helps promote the pupils' own self-esteem and self-confidence. If you are relaxed and smile, it will look as though you know what you are doing and like it (even if you do not).

Commitment   Are you totally committed to the task in hand? Lesson time is not to be used for thinking of the next meal, or when the library books are due back, or the results of tonight's match. The pupils and the lesson objectives are what matters for the duration of the time you are with the pupils. Your concentration and perseverance will encourage pupils to persist.

Empathy and sympathy   Your empathy, and, when needed, sympathy, can ease pupils' tensions, your respect can give them a sense of being important. Your experience of small children or empathy for teenagers can be a helpful addition to the class climate, particularly if you are a parent and the class teacher is not.

Initiative   Using your own initiative is a careful balancing act. There must be appropriate boundaries with your classroom teacher, yet it is helpful if you are able to get on with things without constantly consulting them. Be open with the teachers, and ask if it is all right to use your judgement. Remember, different teachers may want to establish different boundaries. Some may want their pupils to ask them before leaving the room for the toilet, and others are quite happy for you to deal with giving this permission. Some will want you to help yourself to resources, others will want to allocate them to you. Check what is expected of you in terms of behaviour management and adapting tasks. Your relationship with the teacher will become easier with time, as you become used to each other's ways.

Sense of humour   One advantage of your limited responsibilities is that you may be more relaxed than the teachers; your sense of humour eases some of those otherwise tight situations that can occur in all classrooms and schools. A TA can support a teacher who is suffering stress, personal or school induced, for example before an inspection.

Relationships with pupils

Relationships are crucial. Your friendliness to pupils *must* be offered in a professional context, but it could be a lifesaver. You have to maintain a professional distance, not letting yourself become emotionally involved with a child's circumstances while understanding the issues. This may need practice and reflection. One of the problems of being allocated to an individual pupil can be forming too close a relationship. Remember, one of your tasks is to enable pupils to stand on their own feet, to go home at the end of the day, week or term without you, and cope. You need to cultivate a climate of mutual respect.

The pitfalls of having too close a contact are dealt with in the next chapter, under the child protection section. But often a TA can provide comfort to children in stressful personal situations. Parents could be separating, a house move may be imminent, the child may have fallen out of favour with a friend, or have a newborn brother or sister. For the older pupils, trying to cope with the hormone changes of puberty, the TA can become another adult to argue with. Often, simply sitting closely alongside a child gives reassurance and helps their concentration sufficiently to enable them to get on with a task or listen to the teacher talking. For learners lacking confidence, particularly the younger ones, the close presence is reassuring. You must be sensitive, particularly if you are linked with an individual child for several years, and change as they change. Remember that any close contact of this kind can also label a child as needing help. This can be a real drawback to their developing independence. In secondary schools, this presence can become irksome and self-defeating. It will need your close cooperation with the teachers to ensure your presence is helpful and not hindering. You may want to suggest working with a group rather than an individual, working with other children but within call, or placing yourself where you can observe and then move in to help only when the pupil's attention wanders. If you are employed as a 'minder' for a behaviourally challenging pupil, you will need to work out your strategies carefully after full discussion with the SENCO, and where possible with individual class teachers too. One helpful strategy, in primary or secondary classrooms, is to negotiate time in class when you are not directly responsible for the named pupil, but are doing something else and observing the pupil. At some point, you will 'catch them being good'. Make a note of the circumstances, when and why it happened and reflect on your findings with the teacher and SENCO, and, if possible, the pupil concerned.

Relationships with the teacher and pupils

Teachers will make a relationship with their pupils. Adding a TA to the classroom changes the dynamics in a way that adding an extra pupil does not. It is about having an additional adult in the room. MacGilchrist described the relationship between teacher and learner as a pact to which each brings certain traits and experiences. Often this is unspoken but more and more teachers feel confident in discussing what goes on in the classroom with their pupils and in some cases, usually in secondary schools, even asking the pupils to comment on how the teacher is doing. Some secondary schools have even trained their older pupils in using the Ofsted framework. The pupils observe classes and teachers at work, then discuss their findings with the teachers. Certainly, this kind of work reflects confident and constructive relationships.

MacGilchrist *et al.* (2004) suggest that:

THE LEARNER brings:

- Their background

- Their capacity for, and experience of, learning

- Their prior and current knowledge, skills and understanding

- Their learning preferences

- Their current range of intelligence

and

THE TEACHER brings:

- Understanding of the learning process

- Understanding of the teaching process

- Knowledge, enthusiasm, understanding about what is to be taught and how

- Ability to select appropriate curriculum and relevant resources

- A design for teaching for learning that is fit for purpose

- An ability to create a rich learning environment

Together they can increase the learner's:

- Sense of self as learner

- Willingness to continue to learn about learning

- Motivation

- Mutual respect and high expectations

- Active participation in the learning and teaching processes

- Shared commitment to learning outcomes

- Willingness to learn from each other

- Reflection and feedback on learning.

(2004: 91)

In the same way, the teacher can make explicit what their intentions are with the pupils and get feedback from the pupils on how these expectations are best to be achieved. You can discuss your role with the teacher in the first place and if possible with the pupils you work with. You may be surprised by the answers you get, assumptions can be very wrong or at best misleading. It is worth spending time with the teachers you work most closely with, exploring what their expectations of your work are, and how they will enable you to perform to your best. In this way, everyone is clear about your role. When things are not talked about misunderstandings can arise.

First, consider what you can offer to the teacher and the teaching process.

You can offer:

- personal support and partnership;

- adult reflection;

- sense of humour and empathy;

- assistance in creating the learning environment;

- knowledge, skills and experiences of your own, which can complement those of the teacher;

- local background and knowledge;

- an extra pair of hands, ears and eyes;

- what else?

Now look at MacGilchrist's list of what the teacher brings.

continued . . .

Then, together with the teacher find out:

- Does the teacher know your background?

- Do you know their educational background knowledge and expertise?

- Do you have any shared interests or experiences?

- What kind of professional boundaries do you each want to observe in the classroom and outside it:

- What will you call each other in the room?

- When can you interrupt the teacher?

- What responsibilities can you take for changing what you do with the pupils?

- When will you be able to get together to plan and share feedback?

Fox (1998) suggests a simple rating exercise that both the teacher and the TA undertake separately and then together. Her questions are to be answered on a 1 to 5 scale where 1 is rated not at all and 5 is 'very much'.

She asks:

Are you (or your teacher):

- clear about roles and responsibilities?

- valued as part of the learning support team?

- given regular opportunities for planning with teacher colleagues?

- clear about learning objectives?

- deployed efficiently, effectively, flexibly?

- given opportunities for training and development?

(1998: 39)

Now consider what you bring to the learner:

- additional adult interface;

- a listener and a partner in dialogue;

- an individual instructor, under the guidance of the teacher;

- prompts and reminders;

- additional local background knowledge;

- greater flexibility and freedom to spend time with them, more frequent one-to-one contact;

- knowledge, skills and experience of your own.

The partnership of teacher and TA can together enhance the learning experience for the pupil but also increase their own enjoyment of the job. If the learning experience in the classroom is seen as tripartite rather than just a one-way teacher or teacher/TA to learner the sense of achievement for all concerned will be increased. This can but be beneficial. Figure 5.2 attempts to show how joint working of all involved in the classroom learning process can operate.

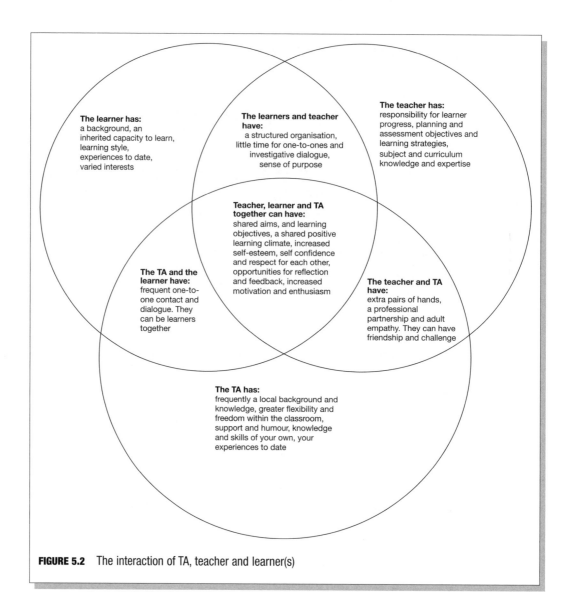

FIGURE 5.2   The interaction of TA, teacher and learner(s)

We have discussed the importance of establishing boundaries with the teacher with whom you are working. If there is a problem, confide in your mentor or line manager. You cannot sort out the more difficult issues; they must be sorted out by the school.

Many of you, particularly in secondary schools will work with more than one teacher and may not have the possibility of forming a proper relationship but do remember those groundrules from Chapter 2 about things to think of when going to a new classroom.

Skills

Teaching skills can be learnt, developed and practised. These are really the tasks that the 2003 Regulations were talking about. But, if teaching is about enabling learning, then the first vital technique when working with learners of any age is to understand something of them as learners. That is why learning had a chapter of its own and came before this one. Whatever the teacher asks you to do with the pupils, after finding out the objectives, you can make more of a difference if you are sensitive to the learner's needs as well.

The interface between learning and teaching is cloudy. A good teacher is always aware of the learning needs of the class, and adapts the teaching programme to match those needs. Those needs may relate to ways in which the pupils learn, or to physical, emotional, social, cultural or spiritual differences. Some of the ways in which we adapt what we do are instinctive, because of our personality. Some of us are better at empathising with people than others are. This could be because we have brought up a family, or have worked with learners before, and have noticed what helps or doesn't. The tendency when starting as a TA is to operate merely as a 'keeper' or 'task minder', ensuring the pupils keep their 'noses to the grindstone'. Your role can be so much more than that.

You do not 'get the children well-behaved, then teach'! Behaviour management is not something that happens on its own. Managing behaviour is about creating a climate in which teaching takes place; it affects everything you do. It is about adopting attitudes and strategies that are consistent throughout both the classroom and the school for all children, not just those who have particular problems. You can develop techniques and language, and practise skills that support whatever the policy is in your school. You must get, read and follow the behaviour management policy for your school. as suggested in Chapter 3. Use the school's strategies throughout the lesson, and throughout any informal times in other areas of the school as well. If you are working with disturbed children, or children who are on identified SEN stages for problems with behaviour, you must certainly consult the SENCO or class teacher for help in this area.

What the pupil learns in the classroom is a match made up of three elements:

- what the teacher wants the pupil to learn (usually based on the formal curriculum);

- the learning style and characteristics of the pupil; and

- the activities of the adults teaching and supporting the learning.

The success of the activity or task depends on an appropriate match of these elements. If any one of these is inappropriate, then something goes wrong. The curriculum can be too hard or easy, the learner can be unhappy or uncomfortable, or the adults may not know the subject well enough or understand what they are supposed to be doing. As a TA, you are not responsible for making the match, but you can assist in all three aspects of the system by understanding more about each.

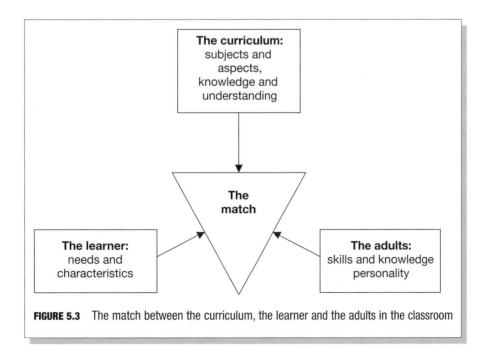

FIGURE 5.3 The match between the curriculum, the learner and the adults in the classroom

Another way of looking at what happens in the classroom is to think of it as a cycle (Figure 5.4), with each part leading into the next. Thus you will be involved in:

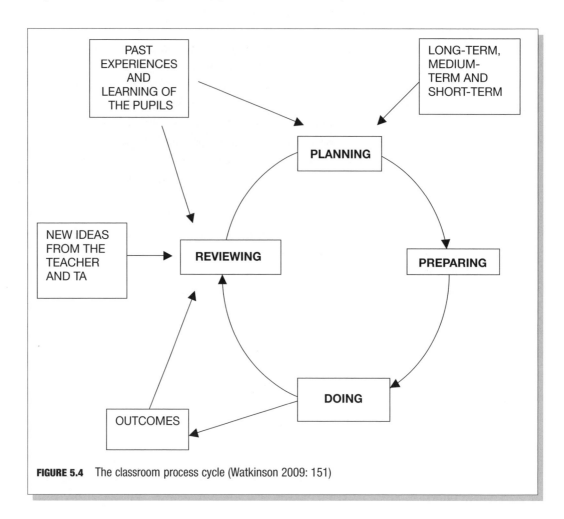

FIGURE 5.4 The classroom process cycle (Watkinson 2009: 151)

Planning and preparation

Before you start in a classroom, you will need to make contact with the class teacher with whom you are going to work. You may be given verbal directions or a written lesson plan to complete some kind of task with the pupils. The task will not be given simply to occupy the pupils but to help them to learn something of value.

Plan: You must also plan and prepare what you are going to do. This includes knowing more about the topic than the pupil does, and knowing as much as you can about the pupil before you meet.

Do: 'Deliver' what you have planned. You'll need to adapt it to anything that you didn't (or couldn't) foresee.

Review: Assess what took place for the pupils and report back to them, and/or the teacher if you can. Clear up, think about what has happened and plan for the next lesson. The learning outcome may well not be the same as the learning intention of the teacher.

Some of you may say: 'But I am only paid for "the doing"', the actual time in the classroom, so when can I prepare or feed back?' If this is a problem you must discuss it with your line manager or class teacher as soon as possible. This book is recommending best practice as seen by the author, which is the practice recommended both by the WAMG (Workforce Agreement Monitoring Group) (WAMG 2008) and Ofsted (2007: 21). Best practice includes planning, preparation, feedback and clearing up time. The classroom 'doing' activity relies on these other items to be most effective. Research indicates that the impact of teachers using support staff is 'compromised by lack of time they have to plan together', the issues being particularly difficult in secondary schools where a TA may work with several teachers in a day. The issue is further complicated by 'the willingness of staff to work in their own time in order to be involved in planning or feedback . . .' (Blatchford *et al.* 2007: 100).

Sometimes the planning seems an unnecessary chore, particularly when you have done it all before and are becoming experienced. But all tasks require planning (even shopping works better if you've made a list) and the better prepared you are, the more smoothly the task will run, and the actual work on the day is minimised. If plans are in writing, then other people can help, or step in at the last minute in a crisis to take over. This holds true for all tasks and activities, including classroom planning.

Teachers have three levels of planning: long-term, medium-term and short-term. Your plans will follow from theirs.

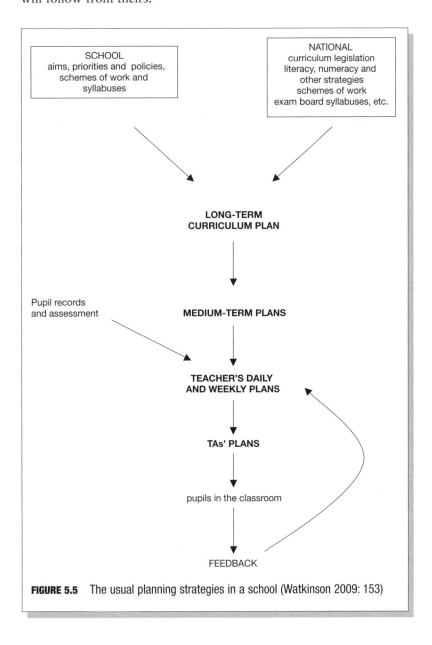

FIGURE 5.5 The usual planning strategies in a school (Watkinson 2009: 153)

Long-term planning

Teachers have a map of the broad areas of the curriculum they have to cover in the school year. Secondary schools usually convert this to a syllabus with each lesson mapped out for the year, but primary schools, teaching all subject areas, usually allow each class teacher more flexibility to plan their programme. These are often based on schemes of work (SoW) published by the government and available on the QCA website. In secondary schools the examination boards used by the school issue syllabi for schools to adapt. The English (produced under the title of Literacy) and Mathematics strategies developed in the late 1990s produced very detailed schemes of work with associated teaching materials. These were first introduced to primary schools and later to secondary. There is more about the curriculum in Chapter 7. Each school will have a policy, including the SoWs, for each subject area that the teachers have to follow.

Medium-term planning

Each term teachers plan in greater detail what is to be covered each week. This enables them to arrange relevant visits or visitors, ensure they have the appropriate resources and books, and gives them an opportunity to review the previous term's work. Thus they can build in repetition or revision of topics the pupils are less sure of.

Short-term planning

Weekly, teachers plan in detail, setting down the objectives of what each lesson should achieve in terms of what they want the pupils to learn. This is where the needs of individual and groups of pupils can be properly addressed. These plans will include what each group is going to do to achieve the objectives, and any other activities such as practical work, assessment activities, and the role of any additional adults in the classroom such as yourselves.

As a TA, you too should plan and prepare and, like the teacher, you can think of your own planning in terms of three levels.

Your long-term planning

This is about your own professional development. Decide how you are going to prepare yourself for the job and what knowledge you need to acquire, both in your skills development and in the subject matter of the curriculum you are involved with. Are there courses that you might take? What reading might you do and what meetings could you go to? Discuss these matters with your class teacher, mentor or line manager.

It will be part of the planning to know what the pupils should be learning from the lessons you will support. Sources of information are the NC, the schemes of work published by the QCA, or your school's scheme of work or syllabus. The national strategies website has a lot of information and resources.

Other useful sources of information are the various staffroom handbooks. If you have been hearing reading, ask for the handbook that goes with the reading scheme you are using. If you are using computers, find a handbook for the internet or whatever aspect interests you. Talk to the subject coordinator or the head of department; they may have some good books to lend you. Remember, your motivation is important to your learning. If you are involved with literacy or mathematics lessons you should be part of the school in-house training in these areas, and have access to the relevant strategy materials. If you are involved in science lessons, meetings of the local branch of the Association for Science Education (ASE) may be of interest to you; they have special meetings for technicians. There is a subject associations website that gives links to all the subject associations and issues some helpful guidance from time to time.

Many local authorities run courses in subject areas for TAs, with or without teachers present, but these may be in the daytime, and you will certainly need to book them through the school.

Your medium-term planning

You need to know more about the learners you will be involved with, and whether they have particular needs or circumstances that you ought to understand. SEN is a label given to a pupil who has some needs that, if not dealt with, will hinder learning. There will be an IEP for these pupils. Some useful and accessible books on supporting pupils with SEN are published by Routledge under the David Fulton Publishers name, for instance *Handbook for Learning Support Assistants* (Fox 1998), *Supporting Children with SEN* (Halliwell 2003), *SEN Handbook for Trainee Teachers, NQTs and TAs* (Spooner 2006). There are plenty of books also from this publisher on specific SEN topics such as dyspraxia, discalculia, Asberger's syndrome, emotional and behaviour difficulties. Another useful book is just on *Supporting Children with Medical Conditions* (Hull Learning Services 2004). Typing your particular area of interest into a search engine will probably find a support association for that condition that will be a further source of ideas and information.

SEN designation usually refers to children at the lower end of the ability spectrum, and those with behaviour problems. All pupils have individual needs. One group not always identified by an IEP but who do have particular needs are high ability pupils, known now under the title of Gifted and Talented (G&T). These children and young people can be emotionally or socially immature for their learning ability and this can lead to behaviour problems caused by frustration. Again further information is available via the government internet sites or a simple book is *Including the Gifted, Able and Talented Children in the Primary Classroom* (Fleetham 2008). Whatever the case, you should ascertain whether the pupils you have to work with have special needs, what they are, and the appropriate way of dealing with those needs in the opinion of the school. You need to be briefed. Talk with the SENCO as often as you can. If you live in the locality, you may even be able to contribute helpful information about the child's background that is new to the school. As you work with the children, you will get to know them well, just by the amount of small group or one-to-one contact you have with them. So make an arrangement to feed back to the teacher any information you have or obtain, in as appropriate, efficient and confidential a manner as possible.

While the class teacher in a primary school will know the children well and be able to brief you on special circumstances or needs, in a secondary school it is the SENCO who tracks the children through the various subject areas and as they go up the school. The SENCO may even be your line manager; he or she will have information on the individual children on the SEN register and will brief you on what you need to know.

Whatever the age of the child or young person in your care, their health and safety must be paramount. Is where you will be working warm and safe? Do you know where to go for help, or what to do in a fire drill? Have you found out what behaviour management strategies are expected of you? Are the chairs and tables and equipment appropriate in the area you will use, and if not can you do anything about it? It is bad practice to find small children kneeling at computers, TAs using scissors that will not cut, adults talking to each other when accompanying a group of children across a road, and poor levels of lighting in the work area. Should there be a real problem, in your opinion, then do something about it as tactfully and politely as possible.

Your short-term planning

It should not happen that you arrive in a lesson as it begins (or even after it has started) to be briefed by the teacher as to what to do or to pick up from the pupils what is expected of you. This is 'seat of the pants' working, occasionally necessary in an emergency, but otherwise to be avoided.

The best practice allows paid time for the TA and teacher together outside pupil contact time. In this way a partnership is built up, relationships develop, questions are asked, and possible problems explored before they occur. This need not be long. In a primary school, half an hour a week is sufficient for a TA allocated to one class. It does get difficult where TAs relate to more than one class, and even more difficult in secondary school, where the non-pupil contact time is usually with the SENCO rather than the subject department.

The next best thing is for the teachers to provide the TA with a copy of their short-term plans for the lessons where the TA is present, or to draw up special plans for the TA. Either way there needs to be a short induction time for the teacher to explain the layout and jargon used. The most important thing for you, as TA, to know is the *objective* of the lesson, and the part you will play in achieving this. (Different terms are used for the learning objective; it could be teaching objective or proposed learning outcome.) Following this will be some kind of activity or task or process that will take place in the lesson. Some teachers then list the pupils for the TA and their particular needs, and leave a space for the TA to write in any feedback. You may change things as you go along because you think it would help understanding, you may undertake more formal assessments under the guidance of the teacher. There is more about this process in the chapter on supporting teaching. You then complete the plan during the lesson, put in any changes you made and why, and hand it back at the end, if there is no time for verbal feedback. Table 5.1 gives a general TA planning format that could be adapted to fit your circumstances.

TABLE 5.1 A general lesson planning sheet for a TA

Date	Teacher ....
TA	**Lesson** ....

Learning objective

Activities
Introduction

Group work

Plenary

Resources

Children						
Individual needs						
Feedback comments						

Any general comments:

Some schools run a simple exercise book system. This provides a communication opportunity for the teacher and TA, where time is tight.

Preparation

Whatever the system of planning you must try to get hold of the information *before* the lesson, then you can prepare. Even if you can only prepare mentally, your participation will be that much more effective. But if you are able to collect resources or find different ones, this will bring your participation in the lesson to life. If, for instance, it is a science lesson on light, you may have photographs of an eclipse, or an old telescope, or a rechargeable torch that you can bring in if you know what aspect is to be taught that day. You may want to do some background reading about a country that is to be covered in a geography lesson, or a period in time for a history lesson. You may also need to prepare the area in which you are to work for an art session. You can ensure you have the right protective clothing for the messy, practical activities, or shoes to go out into the grounds looking for minibeasts (insects, snails, worms and the like) or appropriate kit for PE.

Part of your role may be to prepare materials for the teacher so you will need to find out where things are kept. Do you know how to operate the photocopier, and where the spare paper is kept and how to load it? You may be asked to make audio or video recordings or search for something on the internet. It is not realistic of anyone intending to become a TA now to claim they cannot use computers. Computer use for communication at all levels and as an information and resource source is paramount throughout all schools. Again, make sure you know where everything is, how to operate the equipment properly and safely, how to leave it for others to use, and where recorded material is kept and how it is filed. You will need to know passwords, access and troubleshooting procedures. You must also be clear what the guidance is for any pupil using electronic equipment. If access to equipment and resources is part of your job, it is worth spending a little of your own time familiarising yourself with operating instructions, resource areas, stock management systems, and who to go to for help.

TAs in secondary schools are sometimes required to prepare worksheets for their pupils, in various curriculum areas, to enable them to access the curriculum in that subject. Do check with the teacher concerned before you plan detailed work of this kind for particular children. It needs a great deal of curriculum understanding, pupil understanding, liaison and trust with the teachers.

Properly planned and prepared you are going to make a noticeable difference to the learning and teaching in the classroom.

Assisting learning and teaching in the classroom

Performance

TEACHING IS A PERFORMANCE, an act. All professions have an acting role to a degree. Think of the barrister in court, or the consultant doing a ward round. Being 'professional' means that when you arrive at your place of work, you put the cares of your domestic and personal life as far out of your mind as you can, and concentrate on the job for which you are being paid. It can be a hard act, if things at home have gone wrong, or there is a personal crisis. Some serious crises such as illness of your child, or a close bereavement, may hinder your effectiveness, and some even demand your absence from school to deal with them.

Teaching demands courage, forethought and practice. Be clear about the role you have to play. It is not just 'telling' or 'delivering', it is enabling the pupil to learn something, and not just how to cope with being bored. You will have planned and prepared your material, then have a practice in front of a mirror. Most teachers and lecturers have tried this at one time or another. You may only be doing a five-minute slot to four children on using clay for the first time, but there are still things you need to tell them regarding safety, cleanliness or what they are going to make. Make notes and use them. All good practitioners do especially the first time they do something.

Dressing the part

You will have found out whether there is a dress code in your school. Look at the other staff, if there is no written code. This does not mean submerging your personality; it is preparing your part. Thus high heels may make you feel smart but may not be helpful to the active role you will be playing. An overall or apron might be useful for some lessons such as the clay work, and you will be setting an example to the pupils you work with if you are prepared for this. You will need plimsolls or trainers for PE, and proper outdoor gear such as Wellingtons and waterproofs for any fieldwork.

Culturing a 'presence'

The way you walk and talk should show the pupils that you carry some authority: they should identify you as a member of staff. One of the problems TAs may have is being labelled by the pupils as a 'non-teacher'. TAs have fought for recognition, to prove they are not a 'non'-anything. Pupils pick up unspoken messages of 'presence' very easily. Your words, gestures and stance when asking pupils to do something should convey that you mean what you say and have sufficient authority to say it. This does not mean you should be aggressive. If you appear confident and relaxed, sure that you have a right and proper place in the scheme of things in the school, you will earn respect. Try never to appear nervous or anxious, however shaky you may be inside. Consider carefully by what name you are called. If you are called by a forename and the teacher by a title and surname you are immediately a lesser person – is that what you or the school wants?

Communicating clearly

Speech needs to be clear, grammatically correct, and delivered with a firm but not loud tone of voice. This may need practice on your part. This is not about accent but some dialects may contain ungrammatical words or phrases. This can be a sensitive area for some school staff and it is difficult for managers to deal with if there are problems: speech seems too personal a trait to be commenting on. But staff in school have to set an example, in speech as well as dress. Where the English language is the subject to be taught, correct oral examples do help. You could try tape recording yourself, and listening to it played back. That is how you sound to others. If necessary, you can practise a few simple changes.

Manner and body language

Your manner and the way you use gestures are also important. A lot of subtle behaviour management can be achieved without words. Signalling 'turn it down' can be effective while eye contact can sometimes tell a miscreant he or she is observed, or bring a dreamer back to task. Never appear bored, even if you are, as it only creates an atmosphere of boredom for others. Good manners and respect for other staff and pupils will engender their respect, and encourage their good manners towards you and one another.

Know your audience

Learn the names of the pupils you work with as soon as you can. It helps communication and control, and gives the children a sense of their individuality.

PHOTOGRAPH 6.1 Keeping an eye on children from behind in a plenary session

PHOTOGRAPH 6.2   The TA taking a group on her own

Organise yourself and the pupils

Keep a constant eye on the time if you are in charge of an activity. Give a shape to the activity within the overall time allowed: beginning, middle and end. Recognise the various 'scenes in the act'. Pace is crucial, and ensuring the flow of any task keeps up the pupils' interest.

Performance is hard work, and needs consistency, but is worth the effort. Once you are established in your role you will then find that should something go wrong – say you lose your voice – the pupils are sympathetic and cooperative, and do not take advantage of you.

Explaining or introducing a subject

One thing to clarify early on with the teacher is what you should do while his or her exposition takes place. Do you sit and 'twiddle your thumbs'? Do you sit alongside needy pupils or potentially disruptive ones? Do you get on with other tasks in the classroom or elsewhere? You may feel you need to listen to the teacher's exposition in order to fully explain it later to those who did not listen.

You may be taking a group yourself.

Exposition

Try to put your ideas in a logical sequence, and if possible note the key points. Try to have a beginning, middle and end.

Find the right words, speak clearly, watch the tone and inflections in your voice.

continued . . .

Be sure of what you need to say or do – not too many 'ums' and 'ers'.

Try to involve the pupils. Television presenters try to do this, even without a live audience. Just watch a *Blue Peter* presenter or a newscaster: their eyes, their pace, their pauses. It all looks 'off the cuff', but is the result of practice.

Get the pupils' attention, maintain eye contact when you can.

Use appropriate gestures.

Explain what you are going to do or cover, and what the pupils should get out of it – or learn.

Try to get their interest from the start.

Find out what they already know in the area if you have time, as this provides the scaffolding for the learning you are trying to promote.

Where you can, link what you are saying to other lessons they have had in the same area, or what the teacher particularly wants to do.

Try to make what you are doing relate to what the rest of the class are doing, even if you are working separately with pupils with SEN, to allow them to keep up.

Emphasise the important bits.

You may have to adapt as you go along, so be sensitive to the way in which the pupils are reacting to you and what you are saying. This will help you decide the next step, or how large a jump you can make in assuming understanding.

Use examples or analogies, objects or pictures, maps, diagrams, sounds, anything to create curiosity, motivate or add interest.

Have a 'here is one I made earlier' item ready if that is relevant.

Draw or put key words down as you go along; you may even use the whiteboard or laptop and projector.

Make sure you have paper, pencils, pens or boardwriters if you are going to need them. Do not get up to get things; this is an ideal opportunity for any pupils to lose interest or to become disruptive.

Prepare some open questions to stimulate their minds.

Try to get feedback, and promote discussion again if you have time. Did they understand what you were talking about? Dialogue keeps them both awake and participating.

Respond to them.

Try to leave time to get one pupil to recall what you have been saying to another pupil. This helps them clarify their mind and also gives you an idea how well they have taken things in.

Summarise at the end.

Find a teacher you admire and watch how they explain a point. A mentor relationship with this skill is particularly helpful, where someone you respect will watch you and comment on how you do it. You may even get brave enough to be videoed so that you can watch yourself.

Questioning and challenging

This is one of the most important ways in which you can help children learn, achieve, think, and question for themselves.

PHOTOGRAPH 6.3 Questioning

Teachers use questions:

To encourage thought and ideas:

As children get older, this will also encourage them to challenge systems and values. For some, this may sound like opening up a 'can of worms' they say 'surely school is about imparting knowledge not challenging ideas'. Education is about both for, without knowledge and understanding, any questioning is superficial; without questioning, how can we be sure we understand or make any progress?

Purely to check knowledge and understanding:

Questions may be oral and everyday ('what do you want for breakfast?'), or factual ('what do you know about Columbus?'), difficult ('how are shadows made?'), or instructional ('do you remember what I told you about the playground?').

As a teaching strategy:

Selecting questions that one or two students may be able to answer may be used to break up the teacher's monologue and increase the participation of the group. Watch and listen to your class teacher. They will ask questions at various levels of difficulty to encourage all the children to feel able to answer and thus participate.

Questions that need only a yes/no answer or have only one correct answer are called **closed** questions, and those that could have various correct answers are **open** questions. Open questions require more thought on the part of the respondent, and are sometimes called 'higher order' questions. They need more reasoning, maybe analysis or evaluation of a situation, and usually more time for the respondent to give the answer. In a large class situation there is not time for open questions – but you as a TA with a small group may have the time and opportunity to use them. Questioning, like the other skills, needs practice. If you know beforehand the task you are to perform, you can prepare some searching questions in advance.

Closed questions have only one correct answer. They expect memory recall. Teachers often use this type of questioning to start a lesson that is continuing from another one. The idea is that even if many children can't remember the detail, some will remember bits, their answers will be more interesting and involving of the class than the teacher simply recapping information previously covered. Involved pupils concentrate better. Open questions are asking the pupil to think how or why things happened and not just when or where. Pupils might have their own opinion on things and can be asked to justify them.

You can follow up statements with 'Why do you think that' or 'How does that happen' to make pupils think harder. Then ask someone else in the group if they agree or disagree and why.

Questions

Collect questions over a lesson – with the permission of the teacher – and see if you can classify them. You can do this in several ways.

Why were the questions asked? To probe understanding, to query knowledge recall, to prompt pupils otherwise losing concentration?

Were the questions open or closed or neither?

What sort of answers did the questions elicit? Yes/no? A fact or two? Puzzled faces? A variety of answers, all of which could be right?

How hard were they?

Which pupils could have answered each question?

Which pupils did answer?

What range of ideas was covered in the one lesson?

Asking questions needs just the same kind of clarity, eye contact, and structure as an exposition, but the timing is more crucial. When do you put in the question? How long do you wait for an answer? What do you do if no one answers or if they all call out at once? You may need a strategy such as 'hands up' even with a small group, or you can ask a pupil by name.

Do you correct a child who gives a wrong answer to a closed question, or do you ask others and seek a consensus? What sort of praise will you give for a right answer? What if a child answers with another question? (Listen to politicians, they are adept at this!) Can you challenge the answer to an open-ended question? If you asked 'What do you hope to do at the weekend?', you can follow it up with phrases such as 'Well, what will happen if it rains?'

Children often ask quite difficult question: 'How do seagulls glide?', 'Why is there oil underground?', 'Why is water wet?', 'Why does glue stick?'. Never be afraid to say 'I don't know' or 'I am not sure, how do you think we can find out?'. Finding out the answers together, or sending the pupil off to look something up, or asking an expert, are actions that set children off on the quest for knowledge.

Some questions have no absolutely correct answer but form part of life's imponderables. Pupils will ask at some time 'Who is God?', 'What happens when you die?'. You must think about how you answer these kinds of questions in our multicultural society. Remember you should not give a definitive answer to questions like this even if you have very strong beliefs unless you are in a faith school and it is the policy of the school. Similarly you should check how you answer questions that involve aspects of sex education. There will be both religious (RE) and sex education policies in your school to guide you and if in doubt, ask or refer the child to a teacher.

Observing and listening

Always have part of an ear to what the teacher is doing. Always stop when the teacher addresses the class as a whole, and ensure your group or individual charge listen. A non-verbal gesture of a finger on your lips, or even a look, will help.

Eighty per cent of time in school can be spent on what the teacher or TA gives out, and only 20 per cent spent on pupils actively participating. Again, one of the opportunities for a TA working with a small group is to recognise when to talk and when to listen. You can even talk about listening with the older pupils – how you can all do it.

Pupils appreciate feedback on how they are getting on, but be clear about the expectations of the teacher, so that you do not set too low or too high a standard. It is better to stretch a pupil, setting a higher rather than a lower target, so long as they do not lose confidence or give up attempting what they see as the impossible. One of the most important things you can do, even when working with slower or lower ability children, is to have high expectations of them. Too often they suffer from poor self-esteem – they know they are slower or in a lower set or group and then they perpetuate this concept – it makes for an easy life! Challenge them and praise their efforts. Check with the teacher involved if you are concerned or are unsure how far to push.

PHOTOGRAPH 6.4 Listening

PHOTOGRAPH 6.5 Challenging

Assessing and recording in class

All the time you work with pupils you are inwardly making small judgements. Can they do what you ask easily or quickly? Have they understood? Are they enjoying what you are doing? Should you do it differently next time? Keep these thoughts going, this is the essence of good teaching and will form the basis of the way you adjust what you do to the needs of your group. Occasionally, the teacher may ask your opinion of what went on, or ask you to make notes as you go along.

If you do make notes, remember these are comments about the pupils. Ensure they are accurate. If possible, pupils should know what you are writing about them, and what you are going to do with the notes. All notes should be treated as confidential and either given to the teacher or kept appropriately. If notes are to be used for a study or course, you should have the permission of the pupil to use them – or their parents if the pupils are young – and all names should be changed in any written work you hand in to a college or tutor. This is called anonymising the data.

You may be asked to undertake more formal assessments using prepared materials or structured tests. If so, ensure you are properly trained in their use. Even hearing children read is a form of assessment because you will judge whether to intervene and help with a work the pupil is stumbling over. Many classes now undertake group reading to get more children reading everyday, so watch how this is done and ask for guidance.

The government have instigated a process called Assessment for learning (AfL) as it is so important as part of teaching. The AfL strategy has ten principles. They include that AfL should:

be part of effective teaching and learning; focus on how students learn; be a central part of classroom practice and be a key skill for teachers.

Teachers must be sensitive and constructive because assessing has an emotional impact. We all know how we feel in a 'testing' situation, we do not give of our best.

Learners understand that they need assessing and it can motivate – 'somebody is concerned whether I do this or not'. As some children respond to a competitive situation better than others, beware comparing what you have assessed.

The whole process can help a learner understand what they are doing if they know where it is leading and how their learning will be measured. Unfortunately learning for a test such as spellings may encourage the learning but may not necessarily help the underlying need to spell correctly.

Done well, assessment can include constructive guidance on improvement to learners, not just grade them in some way, and they can be helped to use self-assessment skills. This is especially necessary in the secondary school to enable learners become reflective and self-managing.

So often we 'value what we can measure rather than measure what we value', so it is important that any assessment recognises all achievements. The pupil you are working with may not complete the task set but may have done more than yesterday, or kept concentrating for longer.

Assessment *for* learning is the process of using classroom assessment to improve learning, whereas assessment *of* learning is the measurement of what pupils can do.

In assessment for learning:

- teachers share learning targets with pupils;

- pupils know and recognise the standards for which they should aim;

- there is feedback that leads pupils to identify what they should do next in order to improve;

- it is assumed that every pupil can improve;

- pupils review and reflect on their performance and progress with teachers and they develop skills in peer- and self-assessment.

The processes to be used in AfL should be included in part of the planning.

Test and examination results can inform teaching but they are likely to be much more limited in what is assessed. They are usually referred to as *summative* assessments. The every-day assessment to which I refer here and AfL refers to is called *formative* assessment because it *informs* the teaching. *Assessing Pupils' Progress* (APP) materials have been developed to help teachers determine where children are in their learning using the National Curriculum attainment target levels as their yardsticks. They are available for English and mathematics and will be extended for science, ICT and foundation subjects. You may be asked to use some of these materials. The hope is that some end of year tests will be avoided by the use of such materials although, being linked to the NC levels, they will be formal and summative. Children can then be considered to be at certain levels and enabled to progress beyond them without waiting for the end of a year or a Key Stage test. Also, relevant, targeted support can be put in for the child to help them onto the next milestone.

Using resources or equipment

Make sure you have these ready before you work with the pupils, unless getting out the equipment is part of their task. This may be so in science or PE. Resources should be of the highest quality that is available. You and the equipment, their use and care, are role models for the students. You must particularly take note of any health and safety regulations related to any equipment you use.

One of the problems for schools has been that often pupils had more up-to-date ICT equipment at home. This is less so now as much money has gone into schools to support purchase. ICT suites are now common in most schools, with networking to standalones in class, but even these are now being superseded with banks of laptops linked by wireless connections to a central server. You will need a facility with the various software being used by the school, internet access, email, interactive whiteboards and associated hardware such as digital cameras, microscopes, data loggers and so on. The problem for pupils is less likely to be one of unfamiliarity in using equipment, more one of over-familiarity with certain uses such as chatrooms and games. The schools may also have an intranet for the use of staff. This may have all the policies on it and be a means of communication with staff. Do become familiar with the school's ICT policy, making sure you know all the safety processes, not only about using expensive electrical equipment but about access and use by pupils.

If you are using ancillary equipment, do make sure it all works before the lesson, and know where to go for technical help or spare bits or batteries when necessary. In some schools the TAs themselves are the organisers and technical help for all things electrical. Familiarise yourself with how things work, what associated bits are to be used. Using the wrong pens on an interactive whiteboard, for instance, can cause damage.

With books, school usually has a better range than home could possibly provide. Do not use tatty books; mend them or ask if they can be disposed of. Encourage pupils to refer to books and enjoy them, but also to care for them.

Pencils should be sharp; carry a pencil sharpener and spare pens. Much time can be wasted on these little things. Your care and use of tools safely and appropriately sets an example. Even small children can and should clear up after themselves, and you should leave time for this in your session.

Active learning – intervention and non-intervention

Learning should be an active exercise where possible. This does not mean getting up out of a seat and prancing about, it means keeping brains actively engaged in the task, even if that is listening. Factual knowledge is more easily understood and learnt where we practise its use or application. Literacy and numeracy can be extended by linking activities to pupils' particular hobbies or interests. Pupils find active approaches stimulating as well as useful. Make a game of spellings working as a group, or do an investigation that requires pupils to be interactive

PHOTOGRAPH 6.6 A TA allowing independent working even away from the rest of the class

mentally. Pupils get different insights from taking part, observing one another and talking things over with you and among themselves. Directing a group of active learners takes skill and practice, and the approach takes time and resources. It has to be set against the demands of the timetable and the effectiveness of other methods. A balance is needed and this will be set by the teacher for the whole lesson. But you may be able to adjust how you present some materials, to make them more interactive and fun.

It is equally important to recognise when pupils need to be left on their own to pursue a certain activity. Writing a poem or essay, or recalling an event, may need absolute quiet, even sitting at a table facing a wall. In libraries, tables set out for study often have partitions between them to isolate the students from one another.

When a group or an individual is doing a task, the skill of the TA is to know when to intervene and when to stand back, and how to offer help when requested. You are not there to do the task for the pupil, however small. Give encouragement by doing an example. In art or craft work, have a piece of sewing or draw on your piece of paper, showing how it might be done. When asked for spelling, always get the pupils to try first or to use a dictionary, or even to tell you what the initial sound is. They need to develop their skills and gain confidence in their own ability.

Working with groups

We have seen (Chapter 4) that learners need language and social interaction to aid them. Group work can fulfil these needs, but there can be more to it than sitting them round a table and letting them do their own thing. There will be times when you support an individual child, but remember that working with single children only reinforces their differences, can mean that they miss other parts of the curriculum, and miss out on peer support and challenge.

Sometimes working with a group does mean each one has to actually complete a task such as writing for themselves. You may want to start off your group together and then let them complete the task on their own in silence. But cooperative group work means working together as a group, and children will need help in how to do this.

Nowadays, social interaction in families is much less than it was, and they may need some practice in interacting with one another purposefully. You will need to think carefully about the following points:

Cooperative group work

- How will the seating be organised – in a circle or round a table?

- When may the pupils speak?

- How can everyone be encouraged to contribute?

- How will you ensure they understand what kind of outcome is required?

- How will you bring out the reluctant pupil, cope with the domineering one, and eventually show the group how to do this for themselves?

The group may need a leader and a scribe, and these will need to know what their roles are. Specific subjects may have particular requirements: a craft model may need a variety of skills and tools; a science experiment will need further rules of safety; a cooking project will have to follow hygiene procedures; a debate can be set up as two opposing sides. Your role may be to monitor and report back to the teacher how the group worked and what was achieved. Be sure to time the exercise to allow for summing up, and for clearing up. *Promoting Effective Group Work* (Baines *et al.* 2009) might be a useful source of ideas for you.

Circle time is a specific group activity. It can be formally set up with only those holding a particular artefact being able to speak. The outcome may merely be to allow everyone to voice an opinion. Circle time, if used to explore feelings, needs trained people to lead it, as it could provoke unexpected or disturbing reactions from vulnerable pupils. Discuss this with your mentor and line manager, and never do circle time on your own unless you have the appropriate skills.

Nowadays TAs are sometimes asked to take a whole class but this should only be done by properly trained and experienced TAs who should also be assessed and paid as HLTAs. Being an HLTA also includes many other whole school responsibilities. You should not do this. Keeping a large group on task takes a great deal of skill, and is a huge responsibility. Legally, any adult can stand in front of a class *in an emergency*, provided they do not teach. As we have seen, the definition of teaching is difficult in itself. Thus if the qualified teacher is taken ill, you can hold the fort for a short time until another qualified teacher arrives to take the class. However, if the qualified teacher is present in the room, or sufficiently close to still be called 'in charge' of the class, you may take the large group. This sort of situation often happens with younger pupils, when you read a story or sing with a large group while the teacher does something special with a small group or an individual. In fact, this can be very supportive for SEN children who then get the specialised support from a trained teacher rather than always with the 'other adult'.

With older children, the teacher may set a task for the larger group to get on with, leaving you to ensure they carry it out, while he or she deals with something specialised within call. This is an appropriate use of your talents and their expertise. But you are not a qualified teacher and may not take on a teacher's responsibilities in their absence, however well you know the pupils. You may not be paid properly to take a class, nor might you be properly insured. Even student teachers have to have a qualified teacher present for lessons such as PE. It is also the area where, rightly, qualified teachers get worried about being 'done out of a job'.

Working with individuals

There are some very sophisticated materials produced by the DCSF (2009a) for qualified tutors taking specific coaching sessions with one-to-one tuition. It is a government funded project for children who have been identified using the APP material mentioned above and is very structured. It is part of the drive to more personalised teaching. It is recognised that sometimes there is a block that just needs a little bit of special tuition to enable the child to progress in the ordinary classroom situation. While highly specific, it does encapsulate some principles that you might find helpful when working with individuals. For instance:

- if you have not worked with the pupil before that you introduce yourselves to each other;

- check what a child already knows, easier if you are following straight after a lesson you have both been in;

- check that the pupil knows what is expected of them;

- model the process you are recapping;

- talk about what might be the problem;

- observe the pupils having a go;

- explore any misconceptions that you can see;

- deal tactfully with what you can identify as a problem, an error or a weakness;

- discuss what the problem might be;

- let the pupil practice on their own;

- think of alternatives ways to writing things down or using books that might help;

- watch and praise appropriately;

- review and reflect together on what you have done in the session.

Practical work

Practical work brings together many of the above skills: working with a group, organising resources or equipment, explaining, giving tuition, questioning and observing. The pupils will be active, mobile and as independent as possible. Health and safety procedures must be paramount. ASE (2001, 2006) have produced useful guidance in this for the primary school and the science laboratory and Design and Technology Association (DATA) has helpful information on their website. There may be a copy of such documents in the staffroom. Ask the head of science or the science coordinator to check what you intend, if they have not already given you full instructions.

Pupils have to be taught to use tools correctly and the tools should be of good quality. Even very small children, supervised, are safer with good scissors than blunt ones. But they need to be shown how to carry them safely, and to cut out pieces of paper or fabric from the edge and not the middle. Measuring instruments should be used correctly. Make sure you know yourself what to do and what level of accuracy is required. Are you using millimetres or centimetres? Do you know how to read liquid measures using the meniscus correctly? Do you know where all the tools go when you have finished, so that you can direct the pupils to clean them and put them away ready for the next group?

Pupils may need help in making notes; it is different from writing full sentences. They may need advice on how to make a drawing of what they set up. Clarify with the teacher what is the real purpose of the task to be done, and make the pupils aware of it. Is it the answer to 'find out what happens when . . .' or 'how many do you need to . . .'? Or is the objective to give them experience of certain equipment, or find a way to test?

In art, the pupil may put emphasis on the end product, and whether or not they can achieve what is required; but the teacher's objective may be to explore a variety of media, to find their potential for some other purpose entirely. Self-esteem in artistic pursuits can so easily be dented by an overemphasis on product too early, but can be increased for a pupil who is not succeeding in more academic subjects.

Independent learning

It is important that pupils you are helping do not become dependent on you. If you do the task for them, all they learn is that someone will do it if they wait around long enough. Your role is to enable them to do it for themselves. You must look towards their potential, not just what they can or cannot do at that point in time.

If you can see the potential learning of a child you can put in place steps to bring them up to the next stage. This is sometimes referred to as 'scaffolding'. You can help this process by searching out the patterns and being ready with the right steps at the right time. You may be able to supply a missing bit in their understanding, or find a different word for something the teacher has said, that enables the pupil to understand the content of the lesson or perform the task better. The important thing for the pupil is that you provide the scaffolding, not build the complete tower for them. Seeing what is needed to move a pupil's learning on to the next level comes with experience – from knowing the curriculum objective and the way the pupil learns, and putting the two together. Some TAs have even described 'doing myself out of a job' as part of their role.

Personalised learning

This is the phrase currently used to describe the way in which planning learning should be approached by teachers. Teaching children in year groups using a didactic approach – teaching whole classes by lecturing or talking at them, whether using visual aids or practical demonstrations assumes everyone in the group is receiving the same message and learning the same things. For many years now those at the extremes of the spectrum of capability have been recognised as having special educational needs – those at the slower end of the learning spectrum, or as gifted and talented – those at the more able end, but the silent majority can slip through the net. All children being different, these differences need to be identified and time made to discuss progress individually. Individual targets can be set, and each child made to feel special without a great bureaucratic performance of IEPs that may be needed for pupils with special needs. Good teachers have always done this, but now with the help of TAs and learning mentors, more individual attention can be paid to all pupils in a class.

Combining skills – multitasking

You will soon notice that an essential trait of teachers and TAs is their ability to multitask. This, along with your relative mobility, means you become a 'flexible friend' to the classroom.

You can be a 'gofer' in times of emergency, a shoulder for a child to cry on, anything an extra pair of hands can do. You can be a go-between for a slower or shyer child, or calm a trouble spot where and when it occurs. Because you work with small groups or individuals, you can take account of individual needs in a way the teacher of the large group cannot. You can wait longer for answers, or check progress more frequently.

Try to maintain a balance between intervening and chivvying to get tasks completed. Allow pupils time and space to complete tasks on their own. It is a hard skill to achieve, but is worth every minute you spend trying. When you are observed working in the classroom for appraisal ask the observer to watch particularly for this balance in yourself, so that you know how you are doing.

Feedback

Sometimes schools are not able to pay TAs for time to give feedback to the teacher out of pupil contact time. Fortunately, TAs and teachers find ways and means. Using unpaid time cannot be recommended practice. Informal times such as tea breaks are really helpful and their impact should not be underestimated. Staffroom discussion of children's progress is a vital avenue of communication at all levels in school. In most schools now, TAs and other support staff are recognised as full members of the staffroom. You make a real contribution to the life and climate of the school.

Paper methods have been devised in some schools. The planning exercise book or sheets are used for you to record what happened, or who did what, or how well any particular pupil managed. 'Postits' are invaluable, not only could you attach one to a particular piece of child's work to explain how the end result was achieved, you could put one on the teacher's desk or planning sheets as you leave the room.

As you become experienced in watching children and young people at work, and more familiar with the curriculum, you will be able to make better judgements, not only about how they are doing but what the next step might be. All the observation protocols made in Chapter 4 apply here in terms of confidentiality and care of any documents you complete at school.

Understanding the curriculum

The curriculum

A CURRICULUM CAN MEAN a course of study at a school, but really the word covers everything that goes on in school. The formal part, the prescriptive part that is now written down, is what most people think of when they refer to a school curriculum. But children learn much more than this in school. Probably you remember things you learnt at school that neither the teachers nor your parents knew about – and maybe if they had, they would not have approved. You learnt about other pupils and teachers themselves, about how friendships work, and how to keep out of trouble. These are all part of what is learnt at school. These aspects were sometimes called the informal curriculum and the hidden curriculum. The informal curriculum covers what goes on between lessons: in the corridors or the playground, assembly or clubs; and the hidden curriculum covers the relationships and climate, the way you feel when you work or visit a place. Much more of what was considered obvious and instinctive and used not to be written down, is now overt and described in school policies, particularly, for example, in the area of behaviour management and personal and social education.

The formal curriculum

There will be clear school policies on the formal curriculum covering subject matter and how it is to be taught. If you work in a state school, this includes the NC as a legal requirement in English and Welsh schools. Independent schools are free to set their own curriculum, although some follow the NC or parts of it. The NC is dictated by government, and is an entitlement for all children of statutory school age, 5 to 16. Parts of it have now been rewritten many times with the most recent review for secondary schools being introduced from September 2008. A major review of the primary curriculum was published in May 2009 that has some interesting suggestions for alterations (DCSF 2009b). It is to be followed by consultation and support as to the actual timing and nature of its introduction. Both revisions were the result of much consultation and a result of considerable disquiet about an overloaded curriculum, but agreement about the need for a basic framework. Wales uses the English NC with the addition of Welsh, whereas Scotland and Northern Ireland have their own version. All of this information can be found on the NC website run by QCA. A simpler version can be found for parents on the www.directgov.uk website.

The National Curriculum

Making the curriculum a legal requirement means that everyone has an entitlement to be taught certain subjects at certain ages, and it ensures there is a breadth and balance, coherence and consistency, relevance and differentiation. The NC is:

a framework used by all maintained schools to ensure that teaching and learning is balanced and consistent. It sets out:

- the subjects taught

- the knowledge skills and understanding required in each subject

- standards or attainment targets in each subject – teachers can use these to measure your child's progress and plan the next steps in their learning

- how your child is assessed and reported

(from the parents section on the wwwdirectgov.uk website)

These words are written into the legal descriptions of the NC. All schools will have copies of the Curriculum 2000 document that was one major revision and it is well worth reading the introductory pages (DfEE 1999a, 1999b: 10–13) on 'Values, aims and purposes', and what is required of schools and teachers. The Curriculum 2000 aims also underpin the latest revisions. The four main purposes of it were: 'To establish an entitlement, to establish standards, to promote continuity and coherence and to promote public understanding' (DfEE 1999a, 1999b: 13. The recent secondary revision took into account the ECM agenda and the above values. The distillation used by them and supported by the 2009 Primary Report gives three main aims of education:

enabling all children to become:

- successful learners who enjoy learning, make progress and achieve;

- confident individuals who are able to live safe, healthy and fulfilling lives; and

- responsible citizens who make a positive contribution to society.

(DCSF 2009b: 33)

The original documents laid out the subjects of a NC that had to be studied by pupils in England: these were English, mathematics and science, which it denoted as the core subjects; and the rest as foundation subjects. It aimed to challenge expectations and raise standards and broaden the range of subjects studied. At first, for some teachers and schools, a nationally imposed curriculum was a burden. Schools and teachers had previously been free to teach what and when they felt was appropriate to their school or their pupils. The original documentation was daunting, with a separate ring file for each subject, each formulated without regard to the total burden, any overlap between subjects or the coherence of knowledge as a whole. This did not matter so much in secondary schools, where each teacher is usually only responsible for one subject, but primary teachers usually have to teach all subjects. Here it has continued to create problems, particularly when teaching able pupils in Years 5 and 6.

The NC is for children and young people from 5 to 16 year old. In addition an early years framework has also been introduced for the year prior to the NC. It is expected that all state and independent nurseries and childminders should understand the documentation upon which they will be inspected. There is a detailed assessment and profiling procedure for those approaching 5 years old that should be completed by these establishments or by schools in their first class. These years before the compulsory NC are called the Early Years Foundation Stage (EYFS).

Yet even now, with several reviews and considerably more regulations about documentation, and accountability, England's NC is seen across the world as relatively minimal compared with many other countries. We do not have legislation that insists on the same material being delivered in the same way at the same time on each day of the week, each week, month and year. The national strategies came near to it and were understood by many schools to be so, but they were only advisory. If a school could show to inspectors their standards were sufficiently high by doing things differently, they could do so. We do not have standardised, centrally legislated and produced lesson texts from which we all work. Even so, the materials produced by the strategy team have been followed more slavishly than necessary in some cases, until teachers have become familiar with them and confident to make things their own. Some countries do have standardised texts that are expected to be followed.

There is a structure of years running throughout the statutory school system and four **Key Stages**. Those children who were aged 5 before the end of August became Year 1 in September. If they were in school before 1 September, they would have been either in a nursery class or reception or foundation classes. Legally children do not have to be in full time school until the term after their fifth birthday. There is a real problem for children with late summer birthdays. They are actually often in school a shorter length of time than those with birthdays earlier in the academic year. The 2009 Primary Review has the recommendation that all children should start school in the September immediately following a child's fourth birthday after discussion with parents and flexibility as to a period of part time attendance if deemed necessary. Many schools already do this.

The EYFS describes expectations for children prior to age 5:

- Key Stage 1 contains Years 1 and 2 (previously infants);

- Key Stage 2 contains Years 3 to 6 (previously juniors);

- Key Stage 3 contains Years 7 to 9;

- Key Stage 4 contains Years 10 and 11;

- Sixth forms, where they exist, will contain Years 12 and 13, sometimes referred to as Key Stage 5.

Key Stages 1 and 2 together form primary schools and Key Stages 3 and 4 constitute secondary schools. There are a few LAs with middle schools that children attend for Years 5, 6, 7 and 8. They then have first schools consisting of reception or foundation classes, and Years 1–4 and upper schools taking the older children. Most of these LAs are in the process of changing to the primary/secondary system. Currently young people can leave school at 16+ and get a job, some go on into sixth forms or sixth form colleges, and some young people attend Further Education (FE) colleges. With the raising of the school leaving age to 18 in the next few years this age group's education will become statutory although likely to remain varied.

Until the recommendations of the 2009 Primary Review, the NC from 5 to 16 contained separate subject descriptions. **Programmes of study** described what should be taught, the basis for planning and teaching. There is a framework in a nine-level scale for assessment in **attainment targets** (eight levels and a level for exceptional performance) with **level descriptions** for each level. An attainment target sets out the 'knowledge, skills and understanding that pupils of different abilities and maturities are expected to have by the end of each Key Stage' (Education Act 1996). Each level description describes the types and range of performance that pupils working at that level should show. The level descriptions provided the basis for making judgements about pupils' performance at the end of Key Stages 1, 2 and 3 using standardised tests and tasks. GCSEs (General Certificates of Secondary Education) and their courses were and still are retained for Key Stage 4.

What the 2009 Primary Review has suggested is that 'Direct teaching of essential subject content is vital but not sufficient. . . . There are times when it is right to marshal content from

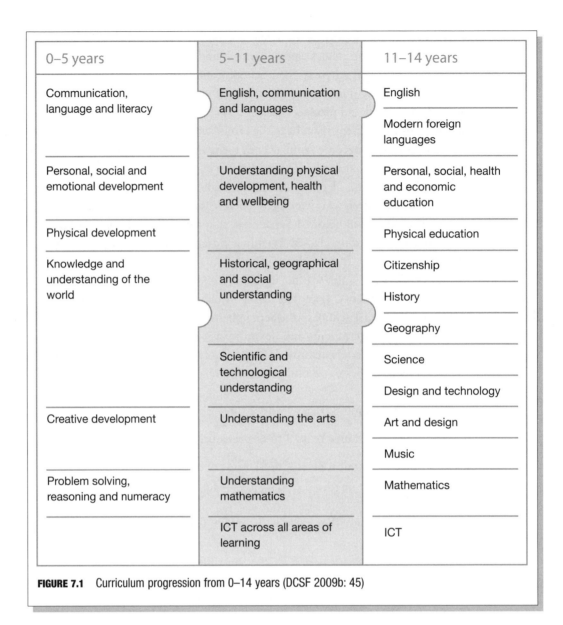

0–5 years	5–11 years	11–14 years
Communication, language and literacy	English, communication and languages	English
		Modern foreign languages
Personal, social and emotional development	Understanding physical development, health and wellbeing	Personal, social, health and economic education
Physical development		Physical education
Knowledge and understanding of the world	Historical, geographical and social understanding	Citizenship
		History
		Geography
	Scientific and technological understanding	Science
		Design and technology
Creative development	Understanding the arts	Art and design
		Music
Problem solving, reasoning and numeracy	Understanding mathematics	Mathematics
	ICT across all areas of learning	ICT

FIGURE 7.1   Curriculum progression from 0–14 years (DCSF 2009b: 45)

different subjects into well planned cross curricular studies' (DCSF 2009b: 16). Hence it recommends that the primary curriculum is organised into six areas of learning. What is so neat about the suggestion is that it not only dovetails with the more subject-based curriculum for secondary schools but also with the broader description of learning and experience suggested for the EYFS. It reflects the way children learn and the pedagogy of a typical primary school. It will provide a curriculum progress from birth to 14. Figure 7.1 shows how the three stages would match together.

Curriculum and subject detail

You will need more details of the subject matter whichever phase of education you work in, greater guidance than is possible here. Do not try to read any of the documents like a textbook. Focus. Choose a subject or aspect that interests you, or with which you are most likely to work. Find the copy of the relevant NC that is in your school or download the bit in which you are most interested from the QCA website. It might be a good idea to start with communication or English as this underpins all that you do. Choose either for early years, primary or secondary phases, depending on what is relevant for you. There will be just a few pages setting out what pupils in each relevant Key Stage should cover. For current primary and secondary phases, attainment targets are in a section at the back of a hard copy. These pages set out what pupils at each level should be able to do. Each subject is set out in the same way. Some subjects have only one part to them but English, mathematics and science all have separate parts – each with different attainment targets. Just refer to them when they are relevant or if you are particularly interested.

Many schools also use the QCA schemes of work (SoW). These break down the detail of the NC into suggested blocks of work, then spelt out into much greater detail giving suggested lessons even. The SoW are also accompanied by a lot of suggested resources so are very detailed. While being a very useful and comprehensive resource, the SoW have rather restricted imaginative approaches and have been heavily orientated to revision sequences for any end of year testing, especially the nationally required Standardised Assessment Tasks and Tests (SATs).

The NC is not just about subjects even though it looks that way. The aims of Curriculum 2000 and the recent revisions are 'to provide opportunities for all pupils to learn and to achieve . . . to promote pupils' spiritual, moral, social and cultural development and prepare all pupils for the opportunities, responsibilities and experiences of life' (DfEE 1999a, 1999b: 11), and are based on a statement of values about the self, relationships, society and the environment (pp. 148, 149).

The QCA website gives guidance on learning across the curriculum:

- how to spot and promote creativity in subjects;

- ICT teaching and learning in subjects, including statutory and non-statutory requirements;

- promoting spiritual, moral, social and cultural development across the NC;

- skills that pupils learn, develop and practise across the NC including thinking skills;

- financial capability, enterprise education and sustainable development.

Teachers, when planning, should adapt or modify teaching and/or learning approaches and materials to provide all pupils with opportunities to succeed, by:

- setting appropriate challenges;

- providing for the diversity of pupils' needs;

- providing for pupils with special educational needs;

- providing support for pupils for whom English is an additional language.

Curriculum for the under-5s

Legally, of course, children do not have to be in any setting outside the home until the term in which they have their fifth birthday. The *Statutory Framework for the Early Years Foundation Stage* came in from September 2008, setting the standards for learning, development and care for children from birth to 5 (DCSF 2007b). The ECM agenda underpins the whole new framework. The aim is to set standards, provide for equality of opportunity, create a framework for partnership working, improve quality and consistency, and lay a secure foundation for future learning. It gives both the legal framework and practice guidance. It can be downloaded from www.standards.dfes.gov.uk; www.teachernet.gov.uk/publications or www.everychildmatters.gov.uk.

The four distinct but complementary themes running through the document are:

- **A unique child** – recognises that every child is a competent learner from birth who can be resilient, capable, confident and self-assured. The commitments are focused around development; inclusion; safety; and health and well-being.

- **Positive relationships** – describes how children learn to be strong and independent from a base of loving and secure relationships with parents and/or a key person. The commitments are focused around respect; partnership with parents; supporting learning; and the role of the key person.

- **Enabling environments** explains that the environment plays a key role in supporting and extending children's development and learning. The commitments are focused around observation, assessment and planning; support for every child; the learning environment; and the wider context – transitions, continuity and multi-agency working.

- **Learning and development** recognises that children develop and learn in different ways and at different rates, and that all areas of learning and development are interconnected.

The early learning goals are set out for the whole age range:

- personal, social and emotional development;

- communication, language and literacy;

- problem solving, reasoning and numeracy;

- knowledge and understanding of the world;

- physical development;

- creative development.

All through a child's time in any setting the teachers or leaders will assess how the child is progressing but an end of stage profile will be compiled at the end of their time at this stage. This will sum up the development and achievement on 13 scales derived from the early learning goals. This will have to be completed by the end of the term in which the child reaches 5 (or 30 June in the summer term) – which is the statutory starting school age.

If you intend or are working in this sector you would be well advised to get your own copy of the framework for reference. The Appendix 2, *Areas of Learning and Development* is a most useful and detailed guide to support early years' practitioners.

The primary curriculum

The 2009 Primary review of the primary curriculum was proposed under *The Children's Plan* (DCSF 2007a). This plan sets goals for 2020 and is an attempt to be more responsive to the needs of children, young people and their families and yet another attempt to raise standards. Flexibility and personalised learning were also emphasised in *2020 Vision* (DfES 2006b). The other major influence has been the ECM agenda and the recognition that emotional and social health influences the way in which children learn. Much greater emphasis has been put on this area of learning. In the original NC of 1987, English, mathematics and science were named as core subjects, but the world has moved on electronically so much since then that English, mathematics and ICT are now proposed as the core. The statement made earlier in this book that it is now necessary for you to have ICT skills reflects this as well. They are the subjects on which modern communication depends. Without communication there will be no further learning.

The review sets out 'essentials for learning and life' as:

- literacy

- numeracy

- ICT capability

- learning and thinking skills

- personal and emotional skills

- social skills.

Then in each area of learning it describes the aims and why they are important. It then details

- essential knowledge;

- key skills;

- the breadth of learning needed;

- what children should be taught in the early, middle and later stages of primary education; and

- what opportunities there are for cross-curricular studies.

It also gives a non-statutory programme of learning for what is a statutory subject, RE.

It is suggested that this curriculum should be introduced into primary schools from September 2011, so readers of this book until that date will have to use the old subject-based curriculum documents, but you will be in school while the new curriculum is rolled out. It is proposed that this should start in January 2010, so you will be in the introductory stages and hopefully be able to join with the teachers in any in-house training and planning.

The secondary curriculum

Curriculum 2000 has been revised for secondary schools (see www.newsecondarycurriculum. org). Year 7 have been using the new programmes of study from September 2008, Year 8 from September 2009 and Year 9 from September 2010. Citizenship and PE begin implementation in 2009 and English, mathematics and ICT in 2010. Details can be found on the QCA website. It will have less prescribed content than Curriculum 2000, enabling schools to be more flexible in determining their own emphases. The purpose is again to help raise standards and help learners 'meet the challenges of our fast changing world' (QCA 2008). The authors suggest their

challenge is to create a curriculum that:

- raises achievement in all subjects particularly English and mathematics

- equips learners with the personal, learning and thinking skills they will need to succeed in education, life and work

- motivates and engages learners

- enables a smooth progression from primary through secondary and beyond

- encourages more young people to go on to further and higher education

- gives schools flexibility to tailor learning to individual and local needs

- ensures that assessment supports effective teaching and learning

- provides more opportunities for focussed support and challenge where needed.

(QCA 2008)

A new set of aims that incorporates the ECM outcomes has been the starting point for the changes.

The curriculum should enable all young people to become:

- **successful learners** who enjoy learning, make progress and achieve

- **confident individuals** who are able to live safe, healthy and fulfilling lives

- **responsible citizens** who make a positive contribution to society.

(QCA 2007: 6)

The level descriptions have been changed so that they fit with the new programmes of study. The QCA website has links to each subject to download the new programmes of study, or hard copy can be ordered from www.orderline.qca.org.uk

Curriculum 2000 (DfEE 1999a, 1999b) will remain relevant for those students not affected by the categories mentioned above and for those in primary schools until the primary revisions are implemented. This is likely to be in September 2010 and beyond.

Cross-curriculum dimensions were identified in the early 1990s but were rarely used by schools. These have been revived in the 2008 secondary curriculum under slightly different titles. It is important for learners to see where what they are learning in school fits into the real world, otherwise it becomes a pointless exercise. The real world is complex and subjects interlink, so the cross-curriculum links are an attempt to make sense of the school subjects. The new list of cross-curricular dimensions includes:

- identity and cultural diversity

- healthy lifestyles

- community participation

- enterprise

- global dimension and sustainable development

- technology and the media

- creativity and critical thinking.

(QCA 2008)

The new curriculum also identifies the skills that young people need apart from those that relate to specific subjects. These include the functional skills of English, mathematics and ICT and the personal, learning and thinking skills. These latter are identified as enabling young people to become:

- independent enquirers

- creative thinkers

- reflective learners

- team workers

- self-managers

- effective participators.

(QCA 2008)

Key Stage 3 compulsory National Curriculum subjects are:

- English

- Maths

- Science

- Design and technology

- ICT

- History

- Geography

- Modern foreign languages

- Art and design

- Music

- Citizenship

- PE.

Schools also have to provide:

- Careers education and guidance (during Year 9)

- Sex and Relationship Education (SRE)

- RE.

Parents can choose to withdraw their child from all or part of the RE curriculum and the non-statutory elements of SRE. Depending on the school, there may also be lessons in personal, social and health education (PSHE).

During Year 9 young people will choose which subjects they will study at Key Stage 4. Their studies in many of these subjects will lead to nationally recognised qualifications, such as GCSEs and vocational qualifications. They choose subjects they enjoy and can do well in, but also try to get a balance of subjects to give them more options when deciding on courses and jobs in the future.

In Key Stage 4, young people have to study a mix of compulsory and optional subjects:

- English

- Maths

- Science

- ICT

- PE

- Citizenship.

In addition, pupils have to take careers education and work-related learning. Schools must also offer RE, SRE and at least one subject from each of the four 'entitlement' areas:

- Arts subjects

- Design and technology

- Humanities

- Modern foreign languages.

The strategies

After the subject definitions in the NC of what must be taught came the twin strategies for literacy and numeracy in 1997 and 1998. As the strategies planned for teachers to use additional adults in their classrooms, many extra TAs were employed, especially to work in supporting pupils in these areas. English includes literacy – reading and writing – but it also includes speaking and listening. Unfortunately, the strategies resulted in a much more formal teaching approach to the subjects, with suggested structure to lessons and, in the case of the original literacy material, even recommended times to be taken over each part of the lesson. However, it was up to the discretion of the school to determine the way in which these strategies are used in other subjects, additional experiences beyond those set out, the style of resources used and the time of day that these subjects take place. It may be worth getting a copy of the handbooks for yourselves but as there is so much additional material now available online, some of which is written especially for TAs to use, it would be better for you to surf the strategy sites for yourself and make doubly sure you know what the teacher wants of you.

The withdrawal of groups for specific support can mean children are excluded from other activities undertaken by the rest of the class, although the children usually enjoy the more individual attention and the activities. It is possible that a child receiving specific support in Year 1 may need support throughout their school career exposing them to a constant diet of being boosted and depriving them of other experiences. Hopefully, as you become aware of all that goes on in school you will be able to discuss more inclusive practices with the class teachers with whom you work.

Excellence and enjoyment

The narrowing of the curriculum that occurred after the introduction of the strategies was well recognised. Schools were timing lessons, giving too much emphasis to technical aspects of English and mathematics without enabling children to consolidate their learning, and having little contextual relevance. The light went out of teachers' eyes and this knocked on to the pupils. As a response to the straight-jacketing effect of the formal aspects of the strategies, a more flexible Primary Strategy was introduced in 2003 (DfES 2003b) especially to try to get teachers to relax. It encouraged schools to be more innovative and develop a broader and richer curriculum. It was called *Excellence and Enjoyment*, and was accompanied by a lot of supporting materials (DfES 2004b, 2004c). Leading on from this, the current directives are to return to a topic and thematic-based curriculum for all the foundation subjects to ensure that English and mathematical skills are well taught, both separately and in the context of the other subjects. This approach has now been fully incorporated into the suggestions on the 2009 Primary Review. In the new secondary curriculum assessment procedures, teachers are encouraged to assess areas such as English and mathematics in other subjects where possible and to link and plan subjects together to prevent overlap as well as make taught matters more interesting and relevant.

There are some general teaching requirements. One is that

> pupils should be taught in all subjects to express themselves correctly and appropriately and to read accurately and with understanding. Since standard English, spoken and written, is the predominant language in which knowledge and skills are taught and learned, pupils should be taught to recognise and use standard English.

> (from the curriculum section of the QCA website)

This could cause you a bit of heartache if your own written or even spoken English is not grammatically correct. English could also be an additional language for you if you were brought up in another country and you may feel a bit insecure about your English knowledge. If you are concerned about this aspect of your work with pupils, do discuss it with your line manager. There are more details about available courses in the final chapter.

Pupils should also 'be given opportunities to apply and develop their ICT capability through the use of ICT tools to support their language in all subjects.' Also, in all practical subjects such as science, design and technology, ICT, art and design, PE pupils should be taught about health and safety requirements, and about hazards, risks and risk control. Again, if you are not sure what these are you must find out before you undertake to support pupils in these subjects. You must know what to do yourself as well as helping the children to recognise and deal properly with tools, equipment and materials in different environments.

Other aspects of the formal curriculum

Schools have to have policies for sex education and behaviour management and can set out anything else they want to teach in their prospectuses. They are also supposed to set out how they intend to teach the formal curriculum. Some books talk about 'delivering' the curriculum, but, to use the old saying, 'You can take a horse to water but you cannot make it drink'. Children and young people are not containers to be filled with knowledge. Delivery alone is not enough, the contents have to be understood and used. You must also recognise the importance of individual achievements, and the value of encouraging pupils to want to learn, to value themselves, and of stimulating curiosity and creativity. It is also important to realise that behaviour management is not a separate subject. If the formal curriculum is taught with the pupils in mind, in an interesting and engaging way, then behaviour is much less of a problem. It percolates through all that you do – you do not get children to behave well, then teach them.

Each school will have its own curriculum policies, laying down how each subject is to be taught, resourced and assessed in that school. If you are regularly helping in particular lessons you need to obtain a copy of the relevant policy and see how your presence fits in with what the school wishes to achieve. If you are in a secondary school, it may well be advisable to consider taking a GCSE in the subject if you do not already have one. This is especially true of science and geography where the technical language is specific to the subject and can be the source of confusion for the student. You need to be sure of your own facts and skills before you can help others, at least one step ahead.

The informal and hidden curriculum

Because the informal curriculum is not set out in legal requirements, every school will be different in what it expects of this area. Behaviour management systems cover this area as well as the formal teaching. Unless there is a consistency of approach – 'this is how you behave when in the school environs' – that is dealt with by any adult passing, the pupils soon consider out of classroom areas as 'muck about' areas and show lack of respect for any adult who ignores them out of the classroom. Where children and young people know that once inside the school gates certain rules of courtesy and a lack of tolerance of bad language apply and are enforced, their behaviour can change as they walk in the gates or door.

One of the results of the ECM agenda is the highlighting of the need for extended schools, providing before and after school activities that extend pupils opportunities. Often TAs are employed to staff these. They may include provision of meals such as breakfast. They provide opportunities to talk with children and young people in more relaxed circumstances.

Things that used to be implicit in the way schools worked are becoming more and more explicit, so less is 'hidden'. Things such as politeness and care of property used to be taken for granted, but now sometimes have to be part of the explicit behaviour policy. Treating everybody with courtesy, whatever their needs, colour, creed or race is spelt out in equal opportunities and anti-discrimination policies. Enjoyment and attitude are all part of a school's culture and climate. Emotional development and behaviour of learners is reported

Consider what you might mean by a healthy school

This can be done by yourself, with your teacher/mentor or with a group of colleagues.

- First consider what you mean by a healthy person:

    You need to consider body and mind, and recognise that age or physical impairment does not prevent you being healthy.

- What do you need to remain healthy?

- Now, think of a healthy school:

    You need to consider people and buildings, and recognise that age or disadvantage does not prevent the school being healthy.

- What does the school need to remain healthy?

Some questions you can ask about the informal curriculum

What clubs does the school run?

Are they in school time or after school?

Do I come to assembly? Where do I sit?

Are there places in the school where the pupils are not allowed?

Are there separate rules for the playground or the dining hall, cloakrooms or toilet areas?

What happens at wet playtimes?

What is put on walls or display shelves? Why?

on, as well as the learners' spiritual, moral, social and cultural development and their ability to stay safe and healthy. An Ofsted inspection of a school recognises these less definable areas, and other aspects of personal development.

You know, when visiting schools, maybe on your first visit to the school you are thinking of working in, that schools have a climate. They try to define this in words, describing their 'ethos', but it is hard to legislate for happiness. While 'to be a happy place' cannot be the first aim of a school (we could say that about homes or social clubs), pupils will not learn if they are unhappy and staff will not work with a will if they are miserable. Once you are a member of staff you will also be part of that school and a little responsible for its climate.

Freiberg and Stein (1999) said:

> School climate is the heart and soul of a school. It is about that essence of a school that leads a child, a teacher, an administrator, a staff member to love the school and look forward to being there each day. School climate is about that quality of a school that helps each person feel personal worth, dignity and importance while simultaneously helping create a sense of belonging to something beyond ourselves. The climate of a school can foster resilience or become a risk factor in the lives of people who work and learn in a place called school.
>
> (1999: 11)

It is about creating a healthy learning environment in the widest sense of the term healthy. It is about taking responsibility for one's own actions and the actions of others – for pupils as well as staff – and can lead to significant and measurable changes in attainment. Keep your eyes and ears open for ways you can contribute to this hidden curriculum.

PSHE and the learning environment

It is also much more widely recognised that the climate and environment in which pupils learn affects their learning. Concerns about the emotional and social aspects of school work, the importance of pupils' self-esteem, motivation and self confidence are all much more prominent. In 2009, there is a consultation on the more formal aspects of the PSHE curriculum that will become mandatory. Concern about immigrants and looked-after children, who all find settling into school difficult and do not achieve as well as their peers, is also being addressed. You can be very useful in supporting such pupils when they come into a school, giving them a little bit of extra attention, helping teachers understand their diverse needs and backgrounds. TAs who themselves come from different cultural or ethnic backgrounds can be especially helpful. There will be a policy for helping EAL pupils. If you are such a TA you will need to understand when it is useful to use your first language and how to help the pupil concerned develop their facility in English.

Partly as a result of the ECM agenda and partly because of the generally recognised need that good PSHE education can support the more formal subject-orientated part of the curriculum, schools now spend defined times on this aspect and it is becoming more mandatory. PSHE includes obvious health and safety things and sex education, but is also about attitudes to life and learning. How we feel about things affects how we deal with them. So controlling our feelings, particularly for teenagers, is a crucial part of growing up and making the most of what schools can offer. There is more about emotional development in the chapter on learning. The SEAL material is worth looking at even if the school you are working in does not use it, if only to understand more how you can talk with pupils about how they approach a task.

The SEAL programme offers seven themes, one for each year of primary school. It is a whole school approach, to help children develop skills of self-awareness, managing feelings, motivation, empathy and social skills. The seven themes are:

New beginnings

Getting on and falling out

Say no to bullying

Going for goals!

Good to be me

Relationships

Changes.

The secondary pack has a full programme of four themes for Year 7. More information, including some material for parents, can be found on the DCSF standards website.

Outside the classroom

The informal curriculum also includes policies covering the environment of the school, inside and out. Most schools display pupils' work and many have a formal policy saying why and how it should be displayed. It may be part of your job to help mount these displays. You will need to get to know the style used and the materials. There are techniques of mounting and various display boards that are effective in drawing attention to the work. Work is displayed for a variety of reasons. It is a sign that the school or the class teachers value the work sufficiently to show it off. The quality of the display and the time and materials used can show how significant the work is. Some schools show only the best work, and others make a policy of showing the work of all their pupils at sometime or another. Some displays are to help the teaching of a subject. They can be posters about places or people, or diagrams of the way machines work. Pupils may help in preparing and mounting displays and this activity forms part of their curriculum. Displays can be two- or three-dimensional. Sometimes books or objects associated with the subject are part of the display. Always keep an eye out for displays around the school, in and out of the classrooms, as they say a lot about the school and its attitudes to learning and its pupils.

Outside, all schools have some kind of play area for break times and most have some kind of grounds. Their informal curriculum will include how they want those grounds used and maintained. Environmental areas, with ponds and wildlife corners, need caring for. Vandals sometimes target these areas, but where the pupils have been heavily involved in setting them up and maintaining them, they seem able to influence their outside school contacts, and the grounds stay in better condition. If you live more locally to the school than many of the teachers, you may get involved in helping look after outside study areas. A major part of the *Children's Plan* (DCSF 2007a) is about providing safe but exciting places for youngsters to play.

It has been said that half the formal curriculum could be taught outside the classroom. If you are interested in the outside classroom, or developing areas outside your school building for play or study then look at the *Outdoor Learning Manifesto* or get hold of *Learning Outside the Classroom* (DfES 2006a) which can be found on its own website www.lotc.org.uk. Do make sure if you are taking children or young people out of the school building or on a trip or visit of any kind that you have followed the relevant school guidance.

Another area of interest allied to this is the movement to develop sustainable schools, details of which can be found on the teachernet website.

Outside support and influences

SCHOOLS CANNOT OPERATE as totally independent entities. They are in communities, there are local and national laws and guidance whatever their status. Figure 8.1 (adapted from Watkinson 1998) shows how a learner, a pupil in a school is at the centre of many influences.

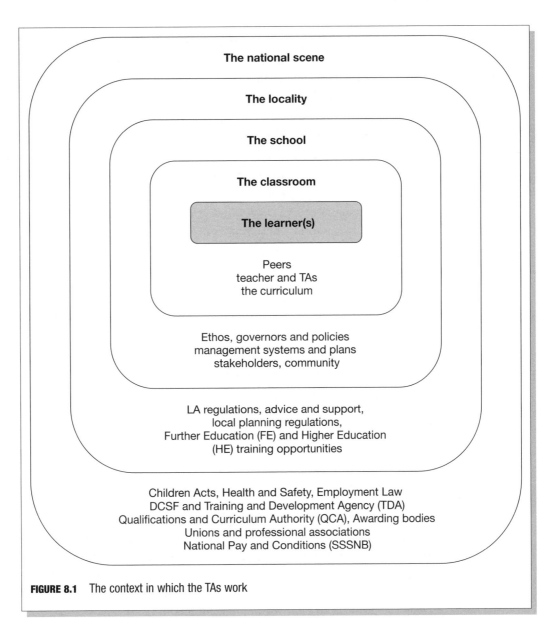

The national scene

The locality

The school

The classroom

The learner(s)

Peers
teacher and TAs
the curriculum

Ethos, governors and policies
management systems and plans
stakeholders, community

LA regulations, advice and support,
local planning regulations,
Further Education (FE) and Higher Education
(HE) training opportunities

Children Acts, Health and Safety, Employment Law
DCSF and Training and Development Agency (TDA)
Qualifications and Curriculum Authority (QCA), Awarding bodies
Unions and professional associations
National Pay and Conditions (SSSNB)

FIGURE 8.1 The context in which the TAs work

Chapter 3 emphasised how you are not alone in the school but must be part of various teams, but you can also see how the school has to respond to outside pressures but also receives support from many sources. Some of these sources are valuable resources for you – especially the training and development sources or various websites run by these outside bodies.

Laws vary in the different principalities making up the United Kingdom, and things such as planning, funding and local support will vary from LA to LA so you will have to find out your local situation if you are interested in delving further. Government determines some basic funding arrangements, curriculum and examination regulations, and laws regulating the structure and maintenance of the learning environment. All state schools have to work within the framework of the NC as well as employment, health and safety laws and the Children Acts that affect all schools. Many independent schools also use the NC. There is plenty of written guidance to help schools operate within these frameworks although most of it is now published as downloadable documentation on the various organisational websites. Most of these documents are published by the government departments responsible for education, or other approved organisations.

The government departments for education have been through several name changes, which is slightly confusing. Thus, the Department of Education and Science (DES) replaced the Ministry of Education in 1964, only to become amalgamated with Employment to become the Department for Education and Employment (DfEE) in the 1990s. That became the Department for Education and Skills (DfES) after the 2001 election. This was split into two departments in June 2007, one dealing with education of children and young people up to 16, the **Department for Children, Schools and Families (DCSF)**, and one dealing with post 16 education, that is with higher and further education, the **Department for Innovation, Universities and Skills (DIUS)**. The DIUS also covered some responsibilities previously held by the Department for Trade and Industry and was reorganised again in summer 2009 as the **Department for Business, Innovation and Skills (BIS)**. One difficulty created by these changes is the information regarding funding and regulations covering sixth forms for those schools that have young people both over and under 16.

Three separate organisations that also formulate policy affecting schools in England and Wales are:

- The **Qualifications and Curriculum Authority** (QCA) is the regulatory body for public examinations and publicly funded qualifications including the curriculum for the under-5s, the NC, GCSEs, vocational qualifications and so on.

- The **Office for Standards in Education** (Ofsted) The new Ofsted – the Office for Standards in Education, Children's Services and Skills – came into being on 1 April 2007. It brings together the wide experience of four formerly separate inspectorates. It will inspect and regulate care for children and young people, and inspect education and training for learners of all ages. You may come into contact with a team from Ofsted at some point as a TA when the school in which you work is inspected. The team will come from a contractor, but Ofsted sets the standards and monitors the teams. Ofsted staff also include Her Majesty's Inspectorate (HMI), who visit schools from time to time.

- The **Training and Development Agency** (TDA) is the national agency and recognised sector body responsible for the training and development of the school workforce. So, it is responsible for not only the nature and standards for teacher training as in the old TTA (Teacher Training Agency) but also the National Occupational Standards (NOS) for TAs. Any national awards for TAs will be drawn up by the Examination Boards, and then checked by the TDA against the national standards.

Relevant Acts that affect education

All schools come under the Children Acts 1989 and 2004 and school staff act *in loco parentis*. The Children Act 1989 was designed to help keep children safe and well and, if necessary, help a child to live with their family by providing services appropriate to the child's needs. Local councils had to provide a range of services to 'children in need' in their area if those services will help keep a child safe and well. The Children Act 2004 was accompanied by the launch of a major strategy document for English authorities, *Every Child Matters: the next steps* (DfES 2004a), which is intended to set the direction for the major programme of change. It placed a duty on services to ensure that every child, whatever their background or circumstances, has the support they need to:

- be healthy

- stay safe

- enjoy and achieve through learning

- make a positive contribution to society

- achieve economic well-being.

This was supposed to mean there was joined-up working between Social Services, Police, the Health Authorities and Education, not just at government or local authority level but in locally based teams. These would be administered by Children's Trusts. There would be children's centres for the under 5s and schools could become the base for teams dealing with the over 5s. As you can imagine such a change in ways of working were going to take time to implement both in accommodation terms and changes in attitudes, management and accountability. You will have to find out how this affects the authority in which you work and your school policies and procedures.

All schools have to conform to the relevant parts of the Health and Safety laws. Among other things, this entails having written policies, fire precautions and kitchens that conform to hygiene regulations. Fire officers and other health and safety inspectors will visit the school to check these from time to time. Industrial legislation includes things such as the Factory Acts and employment law, and covers things such as your use of refreshment and toilet areas and a right to equal pay for equal work. Schools are sometimes anomalies in these Acts; for instance, the Acts may require something according to the number of staff in an establishment. A school can have fewer than this number of staff, but maybe 200 children. Local legislation can be involved in things such as planning permissions and by-laws concerning trespass or rights of way.

Copyright laws govern tape and video recording, photocopying and faxing. Some of these tasks may be part of your job. Usually the school will post extracts from the law next to the photocopier, and you may have to fill in some sort of logbook if you copy material from textbooks. Ask the school administrative staff if you are worried. Assistants support children using ICT, but in some schools they are also becoming the ICT technicians. All schools are now connected to the internet, and most also have in-house networks but hopefully they will have installed all the virus protection required and 'fire walls' to protect the pupils from coming into contact with pornography or other inappropriate sites or chat rooms. If in doubt, check with someone.

Workforce remodelling came about after a major study or teaching practice and procedures by PricewaterhouseCoopers (PricewaterhouseCoopers 2001). This showed that teachers regularly worked more than their contracted hours and were undertaking many tasks that could easily be undertaken by staff with different skills and qualifications. A national agreement on *Raising Standards and Tackling Workload* was signed by government, employers and school workforce unions in 2003 (ATL *et al.* 2003). The WAMG (Workforce Agreement Monitoring Group) is made up of representatives of the signatories, has also overseen its implementation and provided guidance and support to schools and local authorities. Significantly, the agreement does not focus solely on teachers. It acknowledges the vital role played by school support staff and has led directly to the establishment of HLTA standards. The agreement has also helped create other new roles in schools for adults who support teachers' work and pupils' learning such as learning mentors and invigilators for public examinations in secondary schools.

2020 Vision and the Children's Plan

These two documents from the DCSF are worth looking at for their indications of government thinking. They are very readable and even inspiring in places.

2020 vision (DfES 2006b) is a report in the form of a long letter from a group of senior educational professionals in teaching and learning about what they wanted for the future of education. It discusses a vision and suggests strategies to achieve it. It talks of personalised learning, that is more learner centred and the challenges of the twenty-first century. It focuses on the abilities and needs of teachers to bring change about, including the work on AfL.

The Children's Plan (DCSF 2007a) is much more focused on children and young people and the need to balance freedom with safety. It aims to improve the environment and opportunities for parents and children to improve health and well-being. This means tackling provision for health centres and particularly play facilities – supervised and unsupervised outdoor activities. It talks of improving professional development for social workers but also includes suggestions for schools. A further document *Building Brighter Futures* (DCSF 2008) followed, which outlines suggestions for those working with children and young people in whatever discipline/organisation/sector they work. Again, it is an attempt to get joined up thinking.

Special Educational Needs

This is an area that is covered with a great deal of statutory provision (i.e. laws). These are designed to get funding and help to those pupils who have special needs. This is a large area and many whole books are devoted to it. The document with all the current legislation is the SEN *Code of Practice* (DfES 2001). There will be a copy in the staffroom or the SENCOs resource area. It governs all the recommendations about 'statements', IEPs, and the role of the SENCO, and talks much more about inclusion. The intention was that most if not all children except those with profound and multiple disabilities would be educated in mainstream schools with appropriate support. Some LAs even closed all their special schools. This move has met with mixed responses as sometimes the support is just allocating TA hours, which has resulted in the most vulnerable and needy children being helped by the least well trained people. Thankfully, this is now rare and management and deployment of support staff had received much more attention since the Workforce remodelling. One aim in SEN provision is to promote inclusion: this means that all pupils should be educated together where possible, with appropriate support for those who have a special need. The principles of inclusion are well described in the early pages of the NC (DfEE 1999a, 1999b: 32–9). Maybe eventually the label SEN will go and SENCOs will become Inclusion Coordinators.

Simple integration, where children and young people with SEN attend a mainstream school but are treated differentially is not inclusion. You need to look carefully at the provision in your own school and decide whether pupils are truly included in the society of the school as well as the education provision. Inclusion should also extend to all the staff. There should be equal opportunities for all, for instance for staff in access to staffrooms, performance management and resources.

Clearly however, some children have particular needs that need particular support. These may be emotional, social or behavioural, physical or psychological. Whatever they are, they hinder learning. The problem comes as to how best support their needs without excluding them from other activities. Their needs have to be identified and then supported to enable them to participate as fully as possible. Experience has shown that mainstream school does not suit all pupils, their needs are such that meeting them in an ordinary school means they are excluded from many activities, sometimes because of withdrawal systems, sometimes because of the nature of the disability or the type of provision that is possible in that school. Special schools still have their place for certain children and can be resource centres for their surrounding mainstream schools.

SEN pupils used to be labelled by their deficiencies or handicap. Now they are described by their needs. The code of practice identifies four main areas of need:

- Communication and interaction
- Cognition (knowing) and learning
- Behaviour, emotional and social development
- Sensory and/or physical.

Of course, any one child may have aspects of more than one of these categories, for instance poor hearing may well result in communication problems that have led to learning problems. There are also stages of need that can be identified, some of which can be supported by resources within the school either human or material or both. Children are put on an SEN register that is maintained by the SENCO, usually audited by the LA and reviewed with the parents annually. All children with any sort of SEN will have an IEP that will identify the need and set short-term targets for the child to achieve. The child, parents, teachers and TAs (if involved) should all have input into the IEP where possible and thus work together to help the child achieve the targets.

Children who are able to be supported entirely 'in-house', in their own class, are recognised to need School Action. If they require extra support, this is called School Action Plus. Should their needs be severe, then they need to be assessed by an Educational Psychologist (EP). If necessary, in the EP's opinion, there may need to be written a 'Statement' of special need. The method of supporting the child must form part of the statement and the LA has to fund this provision. All the ways of supporting special needs can seem bureaucratic, cumbersome and expensive to administer, with different LAs interpreting the act in different ways. Some authorities have established teams of assistants; others provide support through peripatetic special needs teachers; schools in other authorities are delegated funding earmarked for SEN. As a TA for SEN, your salary may come out of funding earmarked for those pupils who have a special need.

There is also a category sometimes used in documentation and funding streams for those with needs where it is not appropriate to put them on the SEN register, but they need extra resources. They are those with additional educational needs (AEN). They may experience social deprivation, be among groups such as travellers or those with minority ethnic backgrounds or be looked-after children (those in care).

Gifted and talented

At the other end of the learning and achievement spectrum are children and young people who are gifted and talented. These pupils can be underachieving or even become behaviour problems in schools because their needs have not been recognised. Traditionally, such children were expected, by virtue of the extra capability, to be able to progress without extra support and just do more or finish more quickly. Unfortunately, it can be easy for such children to go unrecognised or coast when they could be stretched more. They can become frustrated or recalcitrant through lack of appropriate stimulation or unhappy because their intellectual ability is not matched by an equally advanced emotional capability. Schools are now required to identify such children and to make suitable provision for their needs. Sometimes this has involved TAs as all children, not just those with SEN, can benefit from challenge and questioning or alternative approaches to regular items. All pupils can benefit from appropriate extra adult attention.

The role of a Local Authority (LA)

The government policy of Local Management of Schools (LMS), introduced in the late 1990s, means that much power has been transferred from LAs to schools. Budgets were devolved to the schools, which became responsible for their own financial management and, in some cases, employment of staff. The LA role has become more strategic and advisory: it monitors, challenges and supports schools. Some LAs retain advisers to help improve the performance of schools, particularly those having difficulties. In addition to SEN services (see preceding section), LAs usually offer some form of admissions and/or pupil services and personnel services although they often charge for these now. Library services, music and adult education may still be organised by the LA while services such as school meals and cleaning, planning and building surveyors may be contracted out to the private sector.

Some LAs have special TA advisers, who organise courses, encourage networking, and recommend local qualifications and career pathways. Support staff in general, since the workforce remodelling, have been better served by their LAs than in the past. Do ask where such people can be found in your LA. Some LAs send out regular newsletters to their support staff and arrange conferences or support groups for their support staff that can be very stimulating and valuable. Find out from your mentor or directly from your LA what is going on for TAs in your area – try their website. There are enormous benefits from meeting colleagues from other schools and sharing ideas, and from learning more about children and young people, about the job and about the latest things to help teaching and learning. If there is nothing organised, ask your line manager if you could visit a TA in a neighbouring school, or host an after-school visit from TAs working nearby.

Accountability – tests and data

While most teachers see the NC as a good thing, and parents find it helpful to know what schools should be teaching and what standard their children ought to be able to achieve, with it came a whole lot of systems for assessing children. You are bound to get involved with these. You may be asked to sit with a pupil to read the test paper to them, or practise bits ready for the tests. The externally set tests are called SATs or examinations designed by the examination boards and monitored by QCA. You may help invigilate these procedures or mark practice test papers.

There are obvious problems with tests. Teachers may, and have, ended up teaching to the tests and not to the whole NC. Tests do not show all that a pupil is capable of. Nor can tests be used for all parts of the curriculum. Practical investigational work of science is notoriously difficult to test and, at last, the 11-year-old SATs for science will be dropped from 2010. Many factors affect the results of a test: the weather, the child's state of mind or health, time of the year, the intake date, the child's birthday position in the year, a change of school. GCSEs are

PHOTOGRAPH 8.1   A TA marking practice test papers

not suitable for the whole ability range, and yet the newer vocational qualifications are less recognised by industry or businesses.

Pupils themselves – particularly students aged 16 to 18, or those in the main test years complain about the number of tests and examinations and the boring nature of constant revision work, yet they like the modular approaches of some subjects that get bits of the syllabus out of the way early. Teachers and head teachers recognise the irrelevance of much of the data for comparing school with school. Year groups vary so, a good year can be followed by a poor year making the school look publicly as though overall standards are falling. Unfortunately the ease with which test results can be transferred by computers has resulted in the compilation of league tables and now also underpins much of the Ofsted inspection data. Generally, government has resisted efforts to change the systems but has stopped SATs testing of 13-year-olds and tried to introduce a system of value added data. There are also pilots allowing a few schools to test children when they think they are ready rather than at an annual event. Wales has dropped all external SATs testing.

The collection of numerical data about pupils has made a big impact on schools. You may be asked to type into a database some of the data from the testing processes. New analysis systems have enabled pupils' progress to be tracked in a much more effective way than ever before. Trends, such as whether girls or boys are doing better or worse, can be picked out. Along with this has come the idea of predicting what children should achieve and watching whether it happens. It can lead to setting targets for them that are higher than the prediction, and then aiming to fulfil the targets by increasing the teaching or support mechanisms for a particular child. You may be used in some of the classes to give an extra boost. Additional support materials have been produced by the national strategy teams and can be very successful, so long as the same children are not withdrawn for boosting year after year.

The ease of computers and the internet to deal with numerical and narrative data has enabled school comparisons to be made more easily both by schools themselves and those with a need to know. A system known as *RAISEonline* (Reporting and Analysis for Improvement through Schools Self-Evaluation) is a national database only accessible though a password system. Each school is responsible for keeping its data on this up to date. It has information on the contextual data of the school: factors such as a deprivation indicator, the level of free school meals and the proportion of EAL pupils. It also contains information on the ethnicity of pupils, a census information chart and information about the achievements of different pupil groups. It aims to enable schools to analyse performance data in greater depth as part of a self-evaluation process and provide a common set of analyses for schools, LAs, inspectors and School Improvement Partners (SIPs). It has all the SATs results and information on target setting and national comparisons, along with questions for the school to ask itself.

Accountability – standards and achievements

Schools are accountable to their pupils and the parents and carers of the children and young people in their care. So there will be a system of consultation with those responsible for the pupils both about general principles of the working of the school but also individual sessions between the teachers, pupils and parents or carers. You may be asked to be part of these latter, if so do get yourself well prepared with the teacher concerned. You should not do this on your own unless it has been specifically delegated to you about a particular aspect of the work you do with a pupil.

But, as schools' funding comes from taxation, they are also accountable to the general public on how effectively the funds are spent – that is, on the achievements of the pupils as well as the appropriate use of the funds on various budget headings. Governors should monitor the work of the school in the first place but external accountability is also required. The LA may have a system of advisers and teams of specialists but there will be the SIPs, organised by the LA, who regularly visit the school. These are experienced educators who may carry out mini inspections or reviews of the school but will generally keep tabs on what is going on. They usually visit about once a term – you may get to meet these people or never even notice them.

One of the main documents that a school uses to self-evaluate is again a computer-based system called a SEF – self-evaluation form. It is much more narrative than RAISEonline, which focuses on numerical data. You should be able to see this form if you are interested, and should be part of the consultation on its content. It has sections reviewing all aspects of the schools' work and progress and should be kept up to date by the school. It will contain results of consultations with all the stakeholders and bits of the SDP/SIP. It will tell how the SDP/SIP is progressing and carry comments on the reliability of the data on RAISEonline in describing what is going on.

Ofsted

The inspection service that you will all have heard of – you may even be young enough to have experienced an inspection as a pupil – is Ofsted. They now have a much wider brief than just dealing with schools. Ofsted reports directly to Parliament, not government ministers, which, they say, means they can be relied on for impartial information. Their aims are to improve services, ensure services focus on the interests of their users, and are efficient, effective and promote value for money. One of the better things about inspection is that the criteria the inspectors use is all published and available. It is called the *Framework for Inspection* and there are different ones for primary, secondary and special schools. Unless your school is very new it will already have been inspected several times and all the reports are published in full on the internet, on the Ofsted website.

At some point in your career as a TA you will be part of an inspection. The purpose of an inspection is to form an outside opinion on the strengths and weaknesses of the school. The SEF and RAISEonline form the basis of inspection before anybody comes near the school. The inspectors then undertake a pre-inspection briefing that raises questions in their minds – questions that they follow up in the inspection. There is a great dependency on data, they compare the current situation with past inspections. Subjects are not inspected any more. They judge school effectiveness overall and its capacity to improve. They look at the quality of provision, leadership and management, and outcomes for pupils. Where appropriate they look at boarding provision and provision for the early years. There is also an emphasis currently on the school's contribution towards community cohesiveness. The size of the team depends on the size of the school. There are 'standard tariff' inspections (STIs) that last for either two days or one. Schools only receive a few working days notice of an inspection. Every year, they change the detail of the framework and the data required so if you are interested go online to find these and talk with one of the teachers about what it means for the school.

During the actual visit, inspectors observe lessons in order to verify the accuracy of the SEF data, evaluate the curriculum, assess behaviour and compare evidence about recent progress with learning in the classroom. They observe behaviour at breaks and between lessons, talk to staff, learners and others in the school and have some specific conversations with some pupils to track school processes, such as the self-evaluation and performance management systems. In future they will also talk to 'focus groups' of parents. They look at samples of work, normally during lesson observations, analyse records relating to pupils, such as those with learning difficulties and/or disabilities and looked-after children. They may watch lessons that are managed by TAs if there was a concern or if it was a regular part of school life. As these TAs should be senior, and of HLTA status, you need not worry about this affecting you. However, as part of an ordinary lesson observation they would be likely to watch you at work. They certainly want to know how the teachers and management use and deploy TAs in the school and therefore how effective you are.

A lot of emphasis is put on the ECM outcomes and in future the organisation of the schedule will be reorganised under different headings to reflect this:

- be healthy – for example, helping learners to adopt healthy lifestyles, build their self-esteem, eat and drink well and lead active lives

- stay safe – for example, keeping learners safe from bullying, harassment and other dangers

- enjoy and achieve – for example, enabling learners to make good progress in their work and personal development and to enjoy their education

- make a positive contribution – for example, ensuring that learners understand their rights and responsibilities, are listened to, and participate in the life of the community

- achieve economic well-being – for example, helping pupils to gain the skills and knowledge needed for future employment.

(Ofsted website May 2009)

Inspectors recognise that learning is difficult to measure as such and since the very first framework in 1993, have not attempted to define it. They look at outcomes: achievement and standards, personal development and well-being, and how effective teaching and learning is in meeting the needs of learners.

They currently look at:

- how well teaching and resources across the range of the curriculum promote learning, enjoyment and achievement, address the needs of the full range of learners, including those of pupils from minority ethnic groups or with learning difficulties and/or disabilities, and meet course requirements

- the suitability and rigour of assessment in planning and monitoring learners' progress

- the diagnosis of, and provision for, additional learning needs

and, where appropriate:

- the involvement of parents and carers in their children's learning and development.

(Ofsted 2009: 15)

They should consider among many things: 'Learner's attitudes to learning and behaviour including their attendance, punctuality and enjoyment of learning, completion of tasks, collaboration with each other and engagement in independent work', 'Learners' habits as active and independent learners, displaying consistently good attitudes, learners' development of social and other skills such as leadership, group work, problem solving, speaking and listening' (Ofsted 2009: 13, 14).

Inspectors use four grades, outstanding, good, satisfactory and inadequate. They have separate definitions to follow to determine the grades. For instance, good practice in the quality of teaching is currently defined as:

Learners make good progress and show good attitudes to their work, as a result of effective teaching. The teachers' good subject knowledge lends confidence to their teaching styles, which engage all groups of learners and encourage them to work well independently. Classes are managed effectively. Learners respond to appropriate challenges. Based on thorough and accurate assessment that helps learners to improve, work is closely tailored to the full range of learners' needs, so that all can succeed including those with learning difficulties and/or disabilities. Learners are guided to assess their work themselves. Teaching assistants and other classroom helpers, and resources, are well deployed to support learning. Good relationships support parents and carers in helping learners to succeed.

(Ofsted 2009: 15, 16)

Note the mention of TAs.

Taking this further

Developing yourself

YOUR AIM SHOULD always be to become better at your job. We are all learners throughout life. Good schools are a community of learners, where all the staff, parents and governors are learners as well as the pupils. Good leaders cultivate such a community. Reflect continually on what went well and what didn't and why. Good learners are reflective practitioners – they think about what they do, question both themselves and others.

You can ask yourself:

■ Why did I do that?

■ Could I have done it differently?

■ How do other people cope with that situation?

Look for a book or pamphlet or magazine or a website that might extend your thinking and possibly change your practice.

Discuss what you do with colleagues and teachers.

Share ideas and resources.

Don't worry about perfection – it is not possible!

Even if you have no ambition to progress along a career route you should still take a pride in what you do and develop your capability in doing it. Job satisfaction and quality of practice is high in TAs. As you become more confident you could even become instrumental in forming or helping a local support group. These groups not only discuss matters of pay and conditions but also can provide a way of maintaining your professional development without necessarily seeking further qualifications. Local speakers and advisers can be invited to talk on specialist areas, or matters relating to school developments or social needs.

Performance review

Keep your personal professional file up to date. Whichever direction you take, your achievements with supporting pupils' learning will go with you; your file carries the evidence. More schools are now arranging appraisals or performance reviews for all staff, not just teachers. All staff are entitled to have their jobs reviewed. A job review should have several constituents, shown in Figure 9.1, that repeat over the years.

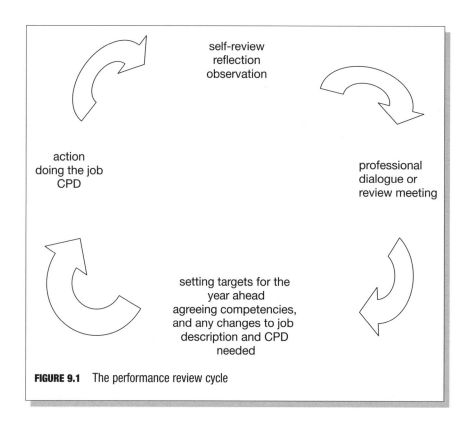

self-review
reflection
observation

action
doing the job
CPD

professional
dialogue or
review meeting

setting targets for the
year ahead
agreeing competencies,
and any changes to job
description and CPD
needed

FIGURE 9.1 The performance review cycle

If you have been keeping notes in your file you will find the self-review easy and you can go to any review meeting well prepared. You could make an extract from these notes to take with you or complete a checklist. Some schools even have checklists for your own use. There is an example here that you can adapt. You keep these notes confidential unless you want to share them. Somebody may observe you at work and talk through with you what they see. If you undertake any vocational awards they will all include time when you will be observed actually doing the job. That was the intention of such awards, they should look at what you can do rather than find out through examinations what you cannot.

This is a valuable opportunity for getting some constructive criticism. You can discuss what you would like observed beforehand – 'do I speak clearly enough?', 'do I explain sufficiently?', 'do I deal with particular children as well as I might?'. The review proper is an occasion for professional dialogue. This is a formal opportunity to discuss your work with your mentor or line manager and to look at how it is developing. The purpose is to enhance professional development, to recognise and celebrate achievements, and to set targets for the future. This is the ideal time to discuss your ideas and needs. Make the most of having someone else just thinking of you!

A TA's work often changes from year to year, term to term, or even day to day if a new pupil with particularly challenging needs suddenly moves into the area. An annual review of your job description is therefore useful for you and your managers. Think about what you already do and form some idea, if possible, of what you might like to do in the year ahead. Your appraiser will have some ideas of what the school wants from you but the dialogue should be two-way. Your wishes and the school needs may both entail you going on a course or two, or doing a bit of background reading.

If you are having a formal review there need to be some ground rules agreed between you and whoever is going to review your work beforehand. Talk with them informally and make sure you each know what you are going to do and achieve. There is a lot more about professional development reviews in *Leading and Managing Teaching Assistants* (Watkinson 2008a: 105–128). Following is an extract that has proved useful in schools.

Possible constituents of a self-review

(This is not something that can be completed in one go. Try it a bit at a time. If you have kept notes as you progressed this will be easier.)

List:

- all the things that you do – how does this compare with your job description?

- your successes and appreciation from others;

- any reasons for job satisfaction and lack of it;

- your relationships with pupils, colleagues and others associated with the school;

- your understanding of the learning process and special educational needs and any gaps you have identified;

- your teaching skills and contribution to the learning objectives of the teachers and any needs you have identified;

- any need for relevant curriculum knowledge and understanding that you have identified;

- your contributions to pastoral and physical care and behaviour management;

- your understanding of and contributions to school life;

- all the professional development opportunities taken: training, courses, meetings attended, personal study undertaken, in school or out of school;

- any personal targets that you have set yourself or achieved;

- any aspirations you have for the future;

- any areas for change, development or improvement – adjustments to job description, and career development issues or ideas that you would like to discuss with somebody.

Purpose: e.g. to try to find out how TAs A, B, etc., actually work with children

Intended outcome: e.g. a synopsis of the variety of roles seen for general circulation among TAs and teachers
Plus individual feedback session for each TA

Protocols   to be observed could be:

- Either side should make comment at any time in the process if there is any discomfort or suggestion about what is taking place or being said.

- Openness, honesty and integrity will help, as sometimes what is left unsaid can indicate issues.

- The main audience of any summary written material will be the relevant TAs and teaching staff.

- It may be that this process might show up matters within the school which need wider dissemination (say to governors), then all participants should agree to the format to be circulated.

- Anything written for this purpose will be shared first with the staff involved so that comments could be made and points of accuracy checked.

- All names are to be changed in the final report to preserve confidentiality.

continued . . .

- Photocopies of all that is written down about any member of staff in observing or talking to them – scribbled notes or observation sheets shall be given to the member of staff concerned. The originals will be kept by the observer securely until the end of the process and then destroyed.

- Individual comments would be anonymised, or amalgamated with others to preserve confidentiality.

- The observation material will be fed back to individuals, who would not be able to change what was seen but could add comments.

- If others are involved, then they would be covered by the same sort of protocols.

- Permission of the parents of any children known to be closely involved will be sought by the school.

- The taking of video and photographs needs separate negotiation.

(Watkinson 2003: 43)

How will the dialogue take place? It needs to be formally arranged, in quality time, but comfortable. There should be open dialogue, but all that is said should be confidential and in an atmosphere of trust. After the interview has taken place, a recorded note of the targets should be given to the member of staff who is responsible for staff development and/or the head teacher. Governors need only know that the interview has taken place.

Whatever you plan to do in the future – whether this is a job you intend to remain in or one step in a career plan – you will need to develop study skills if you want to be a really good TA. Study skills include personal organisation systems, recording information, reflecting on what you are doing and sharing professional ideas. You can practise observing, note-taking, reading, writing essays or accounts, finding reference books and organising your time. Skills improve as you practise them. There are books on study skills, such as *The Good Study Guide* (Northledge 1990) and *Successful Study Skills for Teaching Assistants* (Ritchie and Thomas 2004) that may help.

Personal organisers can be really helpful to start with. Include a timetable of your whole day, not just your school day. When do you eat, talk with your friends or family, relax, sleep? Try to build in some time just for you, even if it is only an hour a week. Try to have somewhere in your home to keep your school things – books, artefacts, your files and folders. If you start a training course you will probably need a whole shelf for the books and materials you collect. Find somewhere to study – to read or write undisturbed. TAs sometimes find themselves studying after everyone else has gone to bed, particularly if you have videos to watch as part of a course. It is worthwhile putting in some time and thought to these practical issues and discussing them with your family. This could save some arguments or heartache later. Begin gently: set yourself realistic targets such as reading a certain number of pages by the end of the week.

Local libraries and the internet can be a mine of information on what is available in your area, and the library may also have useful books or booklets on self-study skills. Try keeping a simple diary, not just of events, but also of ideas and personal comments. Practise indexing any collections of things that you have at home: articles, handouts, pamphlets, especially those that might be useful for school use, such as recipes, instructions, games with their rules, or places to visit. Practise writing letters; we have all got out of this habit with the widespread use of telephones and emails.

If you have a real problem with any of the skills (be honest with yourself) you could consider taking a Basic Skills course. These are now on offer at most Adult and Further Education Colleges. They also have courses in academic subjects, and you may wish to enrol for one if you did not get many qualifications at school. Subjects such as science or mathematics that seemed daunting at school are easier to tackle in college as an adult: you have more confidence to ask important questions when you do not understand. Or you could learn a language that you could use on holiday. The important thing is to get your brain working and do something for yourself.

Options for career development

The TDA website has full information on all the possibilities. A lot will depend on your previous experience and of course your hopes for your future. You will have to consider your home circumstances and your family wishes. Many TAs underestimate their capability and many others are very content to do a basic job with part-time hours and let the future take care of itself. Others have such a lot of responsibilities that they hardly have time to draw breath. It is important for all of you, whether satisfied or overloaded to take time to think about how you perform because you are responsible for the learning of some pupils. That matters. Teachers and pupils become reliant on you as well as your family. Continued professional development (CPD) should be part of all employees' timetables.

As mentioned in the first chapter, there is still no basic qualification needed to become a TA. Remember that at the very least you will be supporting children with basic English and mathematics so it makes sense that your competencies in those subjects should be sufficient. If you have not got level 2 (GCSE equivalent) qualifications in these subjects then a first step would be to get these. If you are concerned about this then look at the www.direct.gov.uk (education and learning) or www.niace.org.uk websites and find a free course in your area in these subjects. NIACE (the National Institute for Adult and Continuing Education) is supported by the DIUS and the Local Government Association (LGA) and replaces the Learning and Skills Council.

CPD can take many forms. The school should arrange for you to regularly meet with your colleague TAs at least half-termly, with the SENCO and other relevant school leaders as appropriate to the subjects you are supporting, and to attend relevant staff meetings. You should take part in, at the very least, three yearly training sessions in child protection and first aid. You must keep up with curricular developments in your field, revisit school policies from time to time and share ideas in developments in interesting ways of working. Legal frameworks change, for instance in health and safety or the kind of responsibilities you can undertake unsupervised. Expectations of what children and young people can achieve are always being revised.

Your own reading of magazines such as *Learning Support*, or subject association magazines, searching for relevant websites for specific disabilities or curriculum information, watching *Teachers TV*, will all give you additional dimensions to your thinking and your work. There are suggestions for further research at the end of the chapter. Make notes, if only of where you found the information of interest so that you can refer to it again in future. Talk to friends and colleagues about what you find out. Just one word of warning about websites. People can put anything they like on the net, including in Wikipedia, providing it does not incite hatred or is pornographic; there is not a review system as there is in established journals. You could be led astray, so do check with someone senior to you in school that you are on the right lines or are looking at a recognised reliable organisation.

Hopefully, you will be able to attend the LA induction training sessions, using the TDA materials (TDA 2006a, 2006b) but, if this does not appear to be an option, look at the materials on their website and talk over the content with someone. The TA files contain all the slides used in the training.

TABLE 9.1 The National Qualifications Framework

Levels	Examples	What they give you (from Directgov website)
Level 8	D (doctoral) Doctorates	– opportunity to develop new and creative approaches that extend or redefine existing knowledge or professional practice – appropriate for leading experts or practitioners in a particular field
Level 7	M (masters) Master's degrees, postgraduate certificates and diplomas	– highly developed and complex levels of knowledge, enabling you to develop original responses to complicated and unpredictable problems and situations – appropriate for senior professionals and managers
Level 6	H (honours) Bachelor degrees, graduate certificates and diplomas	– a specialist, high-level knowledge of an area of work or study, to enable you to use your own ideas and research in response to complex problems and situations – appropriate for people working as knowledge-based professionals or in professional management positions
Level 5	I (intermediate) Diplomas of HE and FE, foundation degrees and higher national diplomas	– ability to increase the depth of knowledge and understanding of an area of work or study, so you can respond to complex problems and situations – involves high level of work expertise and competence in managing and training others – appropriate for people working as higher grade technicians, professionals or managers
Level 4	C (certificate) Certificates of HE NVQ 4	– specialist learning, involving detailed analysis of a high level of information and knowledge in an area of work or study – appropriate for people working in technical and professional jobs, and/or managing and developing others
Level 3	A levels NVQ 3	– ability to gain or apply a range of knowledge, skills and understanding, at a detailed level – appropriate if you plan to go to university, work independently, or (in some cases) supervise and train others in their field of work
Level 2	GCSEs Grades A*–C NVQ 2	– good knowledge and understanding of a subject – ability to perform variety of tasks with some guidance or supervision – appropriate for many job roles
Level 1	GCSEs Grades D–G Key Skills level 1	– basic knowledge and skills – ability to apply learning with guidance or supervision – may be linked to job competence
Entry level	Skills for Life at entry level	– basic knowledge and skills – ability to apply learning in everyday situations – not geared towards specific occupations

Courses are available for TAs at levels 2, 3 and 4 (see Table 9.1). The information on what the qualifications all mean is accessible from the www.direct.gov.uk website, follow 'education' then 'qualifications' to find it. Some courses may be free and others will incur fees. Some may have qualifications attached. The school may be willing to help with fees if they see training their TAs as valuable. Teacher training is at levels 4–6 unless you already have a degree when all you will need is a Post Graduate Certificate of Education (PGCE) if that is your ultimate aim. HLTA training is a bit different. The free three-day courses that may be advertised are not training to be at the higher level but merely training in how to get assessed and achieve the status. It is aimed at experienced TAs who have already been trained in-house to be able to undertake a senior position and whose intellectual ability is that of a second-year university undergraduate (Level 4). There are in some areas supplementary courses in specific aspects of HLTA work to help those wanting to attain the status but who feel they need a boost in those aspects. If you get interested, talk to someone in your LA who organises the HLTA accreditation.

Levels 2 and 3 for TAs are defined by NOS. There are level 4 NOS for those working in management in Early Years and child care. The NOS for TAs are now into their second editions, very refined from the first set and are called Standards for those *Supporting teaching and learning in schools.* They were written by people at the TDA but are published by www. ukstandards.org. Hard copies are now available from the TDA. The TDA website also has some very helpful guidance on using the standards and gaining NVQs. The growth in variety of jobs that TAs undertake has been exponential and the multitude of standards in the pack reflect this.

Standards are based on the concept of competencies. A competence describes what a person can do to a defined standard. (Some people refer to them as 'can-do' statements.) NVQs and similar awards must be written to these standards to get national accreditation. While the purpose of standards is to align current and future qualifications for TAs, it was hoped that they might also prove useful for writing job descriptions and reviewing performance. However, as you will see if you look them up, they take some reading and understanding as they are so very detailed. If you want to understand the content of the standards you will need to discuss them with a colleague, or go on a local course at an FE or AE college. There are books to support the standards such as *The Essential Guide for Competent Teaching Assistants* and *The Essential Guide for Experienced Teaching Assistants* (Watkinson 2008b, 2009).

TAs, when regarded in the light of the standards, can be seen to be **competent,** and this can be recorded. If you are not competent, you can still be trained or helped to be competent. This does not put you in a pass/fail situation.

All competencies are numbered in order that they can be ticked off when observed or assessed on complex paperwork that provides the evidence trail for all NVQs. A competence in preparing a learning environment might be '3.1 *Prepare and maintain a safe environment.*' For this there will be performance criteria – definitions of what that statement might look like in practice, for example '3.1 P3: *recognise potential hazards in the setting and deal with these promptly, according to procedures.*' There will also be some knowledge and under-standing criteria such as '3 K5 *Safety factors and recognised standards of equipment and materials for children. The importance of using equipment that is appropriate for age, needs and abilities of the child. The importance of following manufacturers' guidelines.*' You have to show evidence of all of the criteria to gain the award.

What are your competencies?

How would an assessor know what you do and what you know? How might it be recorded?

- observation and questioning by mentors and other colleagues;

- evidence in planning;

- photographs, diagrams;

- logging activities and use of environment and any outcomes;

- assignments describing the rationale behind the changes.

You might find the NOS lengthy and cumbersome at first, but they improve with familiarity.

Pay and conditions

The concept of levels has also been taken up by the Workforce remodelling teams and a useful publication is *School Support Staff: the way forward* (NJC 2003). This gives some simple definitions of what would be expected of support staff of various kinds in terms of what they do, the experience they should have had, the qualifications they might have and the knowledge and skills they will need at that level. The jobs described are:

- a general TA, at levels 1 and 2;

- a TA supporting and delivering learning at levels 3 and 4;

- a specialist TA giving behaviour guidance and support at levels 3 and 4;

- a TA giving curriculum and resource support at levels 1 to 4; and

- administrative support from level 1 to level 4+.

TABLE 9.2   Support staff job profile summary (NJC 2003: 5)

Expected skill level/equivalent	Induction/basic skills	NVQ 2	NVQ3 specialist knowledge/skills	NVQ4 specialism/higher level TA management responsibilities
Teaching Assistant supporting and delivering learning	**working under direction/ instruction supporting access to learning** – welfare/personal care – small groups/ one to one – general clerical/ organisational support for teacher	**working under instruction/ guidance enabling access to learning** – welfare/personal support – SEN – delivery of predetermined learning/care/ support programmes – implement literacy/numeracy programmes – assist with planning cycle – clerical/admin support for teacher/ department	**working under guidance delivering learning** – involved in whole planning cycle – implement work programmes – evaluation and record keeping – cover supervisor – specialist SEN/ subject/other support	**working under an agreed system of supervision/ management delivering learning specialist knowledge resource** – lead planning cycle under supervision – delivering lessons to groups/whole class – management of other staff
Teaching Assistant behaviour/ guidance/support			**working under guidance delivering learning** – pastoral support – learning mentors – behaviour support – exclusions, attendance	**working under an agreed system of supervision manage systems/procedures/ policy** – pastoral support – mentoring/counselling – behaviour – exclusions/attendance

TABLE 9.2 Support staff job profile summary (NJC 2003: 5) . . . *continued*

Expected skill level/equivalent	Induction/basic skills	NVQ 2	NVQ3 specialist knowledge/skills	NVQ4 specialism/higher level TA management responsibilities
curriculum resource support	**working under direction/ instruction** – preparation/ routine maintenance/ operation – of materials/ equipment – organisational support for teaching staff – support/ supervision of pupils in lessons – general clerical/ admin/technical support	**working under instructions/ guidance** – preparation and maintenance of resources – support for pupils and staff – specialist equipment/ resources – routine invigilation/ marking – general admin/ technical support where some technical/ specialist knowledge required	**working under guidance** – specific support in technical/ specialist area – preparation/ maintenance of resources/ equipment – implementing specific work programmes including assessment – demonstrations/ operation of specialist equipment	**working under supervision/ management specialist knowledge resource** – management team – management of budget/ resources – staff management – lead specialist – delivering lessons in subject specialism under supervision – support special projects – advise teaching staff on specialist area/equip/ resources
administration and organisation	**working under direction/ instruction** – general clerical/ admin procedures – typing, photocopying, etc. – maintenance records/data – collect/record finance – organisational support for staff/ schools	**working under instruction/ guidance** – some skilled work, e.g. WP/ secretarial – routine financial administration – regular interface with public – specific curriculum/ dept. support – record keeping/ production data/ information	**working under guidance** – complex finance – operate complex tasks/systems – management/ analysis of resources/data/ information – advice/ information/ training/ supervision of other staff – skilled PA/WP, etc.	**level 4 manage:** – budget, resource/ systems, people, business, premises **level 4+ responsibility for:** – budget, resource/ systems, people, business, premises

(Reproduced with kind permission of Local Government Employers from the publication *School Support Staff: The way forward* NJC 2003)

The concept of levels has helped the thorny issue of pay scales, but LAs are currently still free to set their own pay scales within local agreements about a single pay scale for all school support staff (sometimes referred to as 'single status agreements'). Local agreements have been fraught with difficulties, especially in areas that left it until the last minute to implement them. Now a School Support Staff Negotiating Body (SSSNB) has been set up to determine national pay scales and conditions of service. It is hoped that having a national framework will bring greater clarity and consistency in the terms and conditions of support staff nationwide than is currently possible and still allow schools sufficient flexibility to meet their local needs.

It will also determine national role profiles and a process for assimilating school support staff onto the new framework.

SSSNB does not have its own website at the time of writing so information has to be gleaned from the trade unions (websites in list at end of book or links from the TDA website), the *Learning Support* magazine, general government websites or local news in your area. The body is made up of employee representatives (UNISON, Unite and GMB) and some employer representatives (local government and religious bodies who run state schools). DCSF and TDA are non-voting members. The views of the WAMG also have to be taken into account. It is likely that the first agreements will take place during 2010.

Whatever is agreed, schools are still free to put you on what scale they consider appropriate for your post. It is up to you to ensure your contract and pay arrangements suit you and what you think you are undertaking. Try to make sure you are paid for out-of-classroom work you undertake whether it is planning or meetings. Remember, you will most likely only be paid hourly for term-time work; there is rarely provision in a TA contract for holiday pay.

Future prospects

In considering your future you may find that a straight TA job or pathway to teaching is not for you. There are many support staff jobs in schools, some veering towards specialising in a subject area or an area of SEN. You may wish to add separate strings to your bow by being a midday assistant or examination invigilator. You may prefer a more welfare nurturing role and opt to be a learning mentor, or become a technician. You may be more comfortable with older or younger children. These will all have special demands, training and probably qualifications. Some of the qualifications would transfer to other professions such as playwork or child care. There is a career development framework publication available from the TDA giving a lot of these details (TDA 2005).

There is also a useful government document, *Common Core of Skills and Knowledge* (DfES 2005) that takes six themes that are common to anyone working with children or young people. Reading this makes you understand that many of your skills are transferable should you wish to go from a school post to one in social work, a hospital or a children's centre. They are:

- effective communication and engagement;
- children and young person development;
- safeguarding and promoting the welfare of the child;
- supporting transitions;
- multi-agency working;
- sharing information.

There are many training and qualification options opportunities available. These include:

- skills for life qualifications in literacy and numeracy;
- induction and introductory training programmes;
- vocational qualifications with units to select according to your role (such as the support work in schools qualifications);
- national vocational qualifications;
- specialist qualifications;

- apprenticeships;

- foundation degrees.

Foundation degrees in teaching assistance probably are the summit qualification for a TA because after that you would go for a full degree in education or a subject. This would lead you to some other occupation or teaching itself. Foundation degrees can often be started with fewer formal pre-qualifications, provided you have someone who can provide a reference that you know enough and are skilled and competent enough to start. They are often part time (2 years full time, 3 to 4 years part time), allowing you to combine academic study with workplace learning, which is their intention.

General principles

Whatever you do, keep in mind some general principles and values that should underpin what you do. The HLTA and teacher standards also include principles. You should be able to show by how you behave, in what you say and do, that you are a person suitable to be employed in schools, to work with children and young people. As a TA you must be a role model and a professional. Read the following, the first part of the HLTA standards (the whole set is available on the TDA website) and aspire to them in your work. HLTAs must be able to show that they

1 have high expectations of children and young people with a commitment to helping them fulfil their potential.

2 establish fair, respectful, trusting, supportive and constructive relationships with children and young people.

3 demonstrate the positive values, attitudes and behaviour they expect from children and young people.

4 communicate effectively and sensitively with children, young people, colleagues, parents and carers.

5 recognise and respect the contribution that parents and carers can make to the development and well-being of children and young people.

6 demonstrate a commitment to collaborative and cooperative working with colleagues.

7 improve their own knowledge and practice including responding to advice and feedback.

(TDA website)

Whatever direction you decide to take, your experience as a TA will be both satisfying and helpful. The role of TA has come from being a hidden and unrecognised dog's body to a profession that young people in school ask about and consider as a career.

Make the most of it – enjoy!

Useful websites

www.ukstandards.org.uk for the standards themselves

www.tda.gov.uk for the official guidance to the standards and most material relevant to TA qualifications and information www.dcfs.gov.uk for official educational information

www.curriculumonline.gov.uk for curriculum support materials

www.fultonpublishers.co.uk or www.routledge.com for useful books for TAs, teaching and learning and SEN specialisms

www.direct.gov.uk or www.niace.org.uk for help with English and mathematics qualification training

www.nc.uk.net for curriculum information and support materials for inclusion, SEN and G&T

www.ngfl.gov.uk for general gateway to educational resources

www.qca.org.uk for support materials, especially schemes of work and assessment information

www.standards.dfes.gov.uk for statistics and strategy materials

www.teach.gov.uk for information on training to be a teacher.

www.teachernet.gov.uk for support materials and documents in general

www.teachernet.gov.uk/teachingassistants for general information for TAs

www.tta.gov.uk/hlta for general information about and for HLTAs

www.nationalstrategiescpd.org.uk for information and publications about the strategies.

Professional associations or unions being used by TAs

www.unison.org.uk – a union for support staff

www.gmb.org.uk – a union for support staff

www.amicusthe union.org/ – now known as Unite

www.pat.org.uk – Professionals Allied to Teaching (PAtT): accessible via the Professional Association of Teachers (PAT)

www.napta.org.uk – an association formed by Pearson Publishing to provide services to TAs

Other organisations in SSWG

www.cofe.anglican.org/ – Church of England

www.cesew.org.uk – Catholic Education Service

www.fasna.org.uk – Foundation and Aided Schools National Association

The main teachers' associations

www.teachers.org.uk – National Association of Teachers (NUT)

www.teacherxpress.com – Association of Teachers and Lecturers (ATL)

www.nasuwt.org.uk – National Association of School Masters and Union of Women Teachers (NASUWT)

www.subjectassociation.org.uk for links to individual subject associations and information of general interest

The main awarding bodies

www.cache.org.uk – CACHE

www.city-and-guilds.co.uk – City and Guilds

www.edexcel.org.uk – Edexcel

www.ocr.org.uk – Oxford and Cambridge and RSA examinations (OCR)

www.open.ac.uk – The Open University

Magazines

www.learningsupport.co.uk – *Learning Support* for primary TAs

www.tes.co.uk – *Times Educational Supplement*

www.scholastic.co.uk – *Child Education* and *Junior Education*

www.nurseryworld.co.uk – *Nursery World*

www.teachersmagazine.co.uk – the government produced magazine associated with www.teachernet.gov.uk

References

Abbott, J. (1996) The critical relationship: Education reform and learning. *Education 2000 News* (March), 1–3.

Abbott, J. (1997) To be intelligent. *Educational Leadership* 54(6), 6–10, Association for Supervision and Curriculum Development, Alexandria, VA.

Adey, P. and Shayer, M. (1994) *Really Raising Standards: Cognitive intervention and academic achievement*. London and New York: Routledge.

Arnold, C. and Yeomans, J. (2005) *Psychology for Teaching Assistants*. Stoke-on-Trent and Stirling, NJ: Trentham Books.

ASE (2001) *Be Safe: Health and safety in primary school science and technology*. (3rd edn). Hatfield: Association for Science Education.

ASE (2006) *Safeguards in the School Laboratory*. (11th edn). Hatfield: Association for Science Education.

ATL, DfES, GMB, NAHT, NASUWT, NEOST, PAT, SHA, TGWU, UNISON and WAG (2003) *Raising Standards and Tackling Workload: A national agreement*. London: DfES.

Baines, E., Blatchford, P., and Kutnick, P. (2009) *Promoting Effective Group Work in the Primary Classroom*. London and New York: Routledge.

Blatchford, P., Bassett, P., Brown, P., Martin, C., Russell, A. and Webster, R. (2007) *Deployment and Impact of Support Staff in Schools* – Report on findings from the second national questionnaire survey of schools, support staff and teachers (Strand 1, Wave 2 – 2006) (DCSF-RR005). London: Institute of Education, University of London and Department for Children, Schools and Families.

DCSF (2007a) *The Children's Plan: Building brighter futures* – summary. London: Department for Children, Schools and Families.

DCSF (2007b) *Statutory Framework for the Early Years Foundation Stage: Setting the standards for learning, development and care for children from birth to five*. London: Department for Children, Schools and Families.

DCSF (2008) *Building Brighter Futures: Next steps for the Children's Workforce*. London: Department for Children, Schools and Families.

DCSF (2009a) *Developing One-to-one Tuition: Guidance for tutors* (DCSf-01066–2009). London: Department for Children, Schools and Families.

DCSF (2009b) *Independent Review of the Primary Curriculum: Final report* (0499–2009DOM-EN). London: Department for Children, Schools and Families.

DfEE (1999a) *The National Curriculum: Handbook for primary teachers in England: Key stages 1 and 2*. London: Department for Education and Employment and the Qualifications and Assessment Authority.

DfEE (1999b) *The National Curriculum – Handbook for secondary teachers in England; Key stages 3 and 4*. London: Department for Education and Employment and the Qualifications and Assessment Authority and the Qualifications and Curriculum Authority.

DfES (2000) *Working with Teaching Assistants: A good practice guide* (DfES 0148/2000 ed.). London: Department for Education and Skills.

DfES (2001) *Special Educational Needs Code of Practice*. London: Department for Education and Skills.

DfES (2003a) *The Education (Specified Work and Registration) (England) Regulations 2003*. London: Department for Education and Skills.

DfES (2003b) *Excellence and Enjoyment: A strategy for primary schools* (Advice DfES/0377/2003). London: Department for Education and Skills.

DfES (2004a) *Every Child Matters: The next steps*. London: Department for Education and Skills.

DfES (2004b) *Excellence and Enjoyment: Learning and teaching in the primary years* [CD-ROM]. London: Department for Education and Skills.

DfES (2004c) *Excellence and Enjoyment: Learning and teaching in the primary years: Introductory guide: Supporting school improvement*. London: Department for Education and Skills.

DfES (2005) *Common Core of Skills and Knowledge for the Children's Workforce*. London: Department for Education and Skills.

DfES (2006a) *Learning Outside the Classroom*. London: Department for Learning and Skills.

DfES (2006b) *2020 Vision: Report of the teaching and learning in 2020 review group* (Review group report PPOAK/D16/1206/53). London: Department for Education and Skills.

Driver, R. (1983) *The Pupil as Scientist?* Milton Keynes and Philadelphia, PA: Open University Press.

Dryden, G. and Vos, J. (2005) *The New Learning Revolution*. Stafford: Network Educational Press with The Learning Web, Auckland, New Zealand.

Dunne, R. and Wragg, T. (1994) *Effective Teaching*. London and New York: Routledge.

Fleetham, M. (2008) *Including the Gifted, Able and Talented Children in the Primary Classroom*. Cambridge: LDA.

Fox, G. (1998) *A Handbook for Learning Support Assistants*. London: David Fulton Publishers.

Freiberg, H.J. and Stein, T.A. (1999) Measuring, improving and sustaining healthy learning environment. In H.J. Freiberg (ed.) *School Climate*. London and Philadelphia, PA: Falmer Press, pp. 11–29.

Gardner, H., Kornhaber, M.L. and Wake, W.K. (1996) *Intelligence: Multiple perspectives*. New York: Holt Rinehart & Wilson Inc.

Goleman, D. (1996) *Emotional Intelligence*. London: Bloomsbury Publishing.

Halliwell, M. (2003) *Supporting Children with SEN*. London: David Fulton Publishers.

Harding, J. and Meldon-Smith, L. (1996) *How to Make Observations and Assessments*. London: Hodder & Stoughton.

Hopkins, D. (1995) The Nature of Teaching. A lecture given at a meeting of the Essex Primary Schools' Improvement. Research Project members.

Hull Learning Services (2004) *Supporting Children with Medical Conditions*. London: David Fulton Publishers.

Kyriacou, C. (2007) *Essential Teaching Skills*. (3rd edn). Cheltenham: Nelson Thornes.

Kyriacou, C. (2009) *Effective Teaching in Schools: Theory and practice*. (3rd edn). Cheltenham: Nelson Thornes (Publishers).

Learning Through Science (1980). London and Milwaukee, WI: Schools Council by Macdonald Educational.

MacGilchrist, B., Myers, K. and Reed, J. (2004) *The Intelligent School*. (2nd edn). London: Thousand Oaks, CA; New Delhi: Sage.

Mortimore, P., Sammons, P., Stoll, L., Lewis, D. and Ecob, R. (1988) *School Matters*. Wells: Open Books Publishing.

NJC (2003) *Support Staff: The way forward*. London: Employers Organisation for the National Joint Council for Local Government Services.

Northledge, A. (1990) *The Good Study Guide*. Milton Keynes: The Open University.

Nuffield Primary Science (1967) *Teachers' Guide*. London: Collins.

O'Brien, T. and Garner, P. (2001) *Untold Stories: Learning support assistants and their work*. Stoke-on-Trent and Sterling, NJ: Trentham Books.

Ofsted (2007) *Reforming and Developing the School Workforce* (070020). London: Office for Standards in Education.

Ofsted (2009) *Using the Evaluation Schedule: Guidance for inspectors of schools*. (April 2009 edn). London: Office for Standards in Education.

PricewaterhouseCoopers (2001) *Teacher Workload Study*. Draft final report. PricewaterhouseCoopers.

QCA (2007) *The New Secondary Curriculum: What has changed and why*. London: Qualifications and Curriculum Authority.

QCA (2008) *The Secondary Curriculum: A curriculum for the future*. London: Qualifications and Curriculum Authority [06.01.2008].

Ritchie, C. and Thomas, P. (2004) *Successful Study: Skills for teaching assistants*. London: David Fulton Publishers.

Rogers, B. (2006) *Classroom Behaviour*. (2nd edn). London, Thousand Oaks, CA and New Delhi: Paul Chapman Publishing (Sage); Sage Publications Inc and Sage Publications India Pvt.

Rogers, B. (2007) *Behaviour Management: A whole school approach*. Los Angeles, London, New Delhi, Singapore, Washington DC: Sage.

Russell, T.L.K., and McGuigan, L. (1991) *Materials*. Liverpool: Liverpool University Press.

Sammons, P. (1999) *School Effectiveness: Coming of age in the twenty-first century*. Lisse, The Netherlands: Swets & Zeitlingeer Publishers.

Sammons, P.H.J. and Mortimore, P. (1995) *Key Characteristics of Effective Schools*. London: Office for Standards in Education.

Spooner, W. (2006) *The SEN Handbook for Trainee Teachers, NQTs and Teaching Assistants*. London: David Fulton Publishers.

TDA (2005) *Career Development Framework for School Support Staff: Guidance handbook*. London: Training and Development Agency for Schools.

TDA (2006a) *Teaching Assistant File: Primary Induction*. London: Training and Development Agency.

TDA (2006b) *Teaching Assistant File: Secondary induction*. London: Training and Development Agency.

WAMG (2008) *Regulations and Guidance under S133 of the Education Act 2002*. London: Department for Children, Families and Schools for the Workforce Agreement Monitoring Group.

Watkins, C. and Mortimore, P. (1999) *Pedagogy: What do we know?* In P. Mortimore (ed.). *Understanding Pedagogy and Its Impact on Learning*. Thousand Oaks, CA, London and New Delhi: Paul Chapman Publishing/Sage Publications, pp. 1–19.

Watkinson, A. (1998) *Supporting Learning and Assisting Teaching: Topic 2*. National Foundation for Educational Research, 20 (Autumn).

Watkinson, A. (2003) *Managing Teaching Assistants: A guide for headteachers, managers and teachers*. London: Routledge Falmer.

Watkinson, A. (2008a) *Leading and Managing Teaching Assistants*. London: David Fulton Publishers (Routledge).

Watkinson, A. (2008b) *The Essential Guide for Competent Teaching Assistants*. (2nd edn). Abingdon, UK and New York: Routledge: A David Fulton Book.

Watkinson, A. (2009) *The Essential Guide for Experienced Teaching Assistants*. (2nd edn). Abingdon, UK and New York: Routledge: A David Fulton Book.

Wood, D. (1998) *How Children Think and Learn*. (2nd edn). Oxford, UK and Cambridge, MA: Blackwell.

Wragg, E.C. (1999) *An Introduction to Classroom Observation*. (2nd edn). London and New York: Routledge.

Index